The Gifts of Infertility

The Gifts of Infertility

A True Story of Heartbreak and Hope

Sandy Hickman

"Many are the plans in a man's heart,
but it is the Lord's purpose that prevails."
Proverbs19:21

WESTBOW
PRESS
A DIVISION OF THOMAS NELSON

WestBow Press books may be ordered through booksellers or by contacting:

WestBow Press
A Division of Thomas Nelson
1663 Liberty Drive
Bloomington, IN 47403
www.westbowpress.com
1-(866) 928-1240

ISBN: 978-1-4497-4591-2 (sc)
ISBN: 978-1-4497-4592-9 (e)
Library of Congress Control Number: 2012906315

Printed in the United States of America

WestBow Press rev. date: 5/10/2012

This book is dedicated to my dear husband. Your love, support, and patience helped me find my way. You are an amazing man and I am so thankful that on this journey of life, I have you by my side. You are my lover, my best friend, my rock, and my biggest fan. I love you.

And I dedicate this book to all of the women who have had their hearts broken and dreams dashed and had to become one of the millions of women who have suffered a miscarriage.

FORWARD

I am not a writer. I am not an expert on infertility. I do not have all of the answers that you may be looking for. I do, however, have a heart to share my experience with you. When I began writing this story, it was merely a healing project for myself. I needed to document my journey. I needed to record this time in my life that had such an impact on every aspect of my being. I needed to record all of the painful details and the amazing way God worked through it. I wanted to be able to read my story again and again and be reminded of what a loving and providential God I belong to. That was my reason for writing my story.

When I was sinking further and further into my pit of infertility, I craved any personal stories of women who had suffered like I was suffering. I found a handful, but few included the spiritual side of the struggle. I feel this is so important to share as part of my story. I am a Christian. I am also human. My experience with the church and the Christian world is that, as Christians, we are somehow taught that by being honest and admitting we don't understand God or that we are angry with Him is a sign of weakness, a sign that our faith is faltering. Let me reassure you my Christian friend. If this is something you are struggling with, it is okay to admit you don't understand, to admit you don't like the path God has brought you to, to admit that you can't see the good that could come from this pain and heartbreak. God knows your heart. He knows exactly how you feel. You can't pretend and fool Him. Be honest with Him. Be honest with yourself. Be honest with those around you. Trust in God, even when you don't understand or like the path He is leading you down. Only then can God begin to bring healing to your heart.

My story consists of two journeys: a journey of despair and a journey of hope. My prayer is that God will use these pages to touch your heart and speak to you. You are not alone in your journey. There are so many women who have struggled with infertility. But I want you to know there is hope, that it is possible to find peace with this monster. I pray that you too will be able to climb out of the dark pit, dust yourself off, feel the warmth of the sun, and be thankful for the journey- be thankful for the gifts of infertility.

"Many are the plans in a man's heart, but it is the Lord's purpose that prevails." Proverbs 19:21

1
THE BEGINNING OF IT ALL

It was Tuesday, May 8, 2001. It was supposed to be just a regular annual appointment with my gynecologist. Instead, it was a day filled with excitement, surprise, and happiness that would be the catalyst to four years of anger, grief, and devastation. This is my story.

My husband, Bill, and I had decided to have a family. It was not a decision that was made over night or without a great deal of thought. We had been married for eight years and were very settled in our life for two. We each had full time jobs and enjoyed spending time together. But I really felt the desire to be a mom, and Bill had finally decided he wanted to be a dad. We assumed that once we made the decision to start a family, it would happen easily and quickly. We had no reason to think otherwise. My mom had not had trouble getting pregnant with my sister and me, and my sister had four beautiful, healthy children that came easily and quickly for her. Besides, that's the way it's supposed to happen. You decide you want a baby and a year later you're changing diapers and getting up during the night and getting no sleep. That's what I expected. That's how I had planned things to go. Everything would be soft and fluffy and have that baby smell. We would delight in telling our family and friends our joyous news and cry as they hugged and told us how happy they were. We would dream of what our baby would look like and whose eyes and chin he would have. We would spend our time painting and preparing a nursery, filling it with cute little toys and tiny little outfits. We would spend time shopping for clothes and furniture, registering for gifts, going to doctor appointments to see how much weight I'd gained and to hear our baby's heartbeat, be showered with gifts, and watch my tummy grow. We would be bursting with excitement as we counted down the days until we would make that trip to the hospital when we would arrive as a couple and leave as a family. It would all be wonderful and filled with laughter and excitement. The most difficult thing we would have to deal with was deciding if the nursery should be decorated in bunnies or in bears. That's the way it's supposed to be. That's what I expected.

Bill and I had met each other during the spring of our senior year in high school through a mutual friend. After graduation, Bill and I spoke several times on the phone and saw each other on a few occasions over the summer. There was something about him that drew me to him. He was so gentle and thoughtful. He was so genuine and smart. I wanted to be around him all the time. I knew I had to take matters into my own hands because he was a bit shy, and I didn't want to risk not going out with him. I didn't want to come on too strong or seem too desperate, so I played it cool. That fall, we both started attending the same community college. Neither of us knew anyone else on the small campus, so we sought out one another to have lunch with and study with and just hang out in between classes. We were majoring in different fields, but we still had some of the same university requirement classes together. We enjoyed being with each other. We laughed a lot. There was an instant friendship from the beginning. I had never felt so comfortable with anyone. I felt I could really be myself, no pretending or playing games. I could be completely honest about things and knew he wouldn't judge me, just accept me for who I was. He really listened when I talked and seemed truly concerned for my feelings. He respected me and put me first, ahead of his friends and his own wants. He made me feel like I was special and that there was no one he'd rather be around. We got along so well and hardly ever quarreled or disagreed, mostly due to Bill being so giving and unselfish. We were both fairly easy going people who strove each day to make the other person happy. We were interested in the same things and thought the same way about most things. We both had grown up in a Christian home and shared the same Christian values and beliefs. I knew right away that he was the man I was going to marry.

Our relationship quickly grew into more than just friends. It was probably only a month, or maybe even less, before we were officially dating each other. I was walking in the clouds! I had found the perfect man. (perfect for me, anyway!) I knew, even from those very early days, he would be fully committed to me and would take care of me. He made me feel safe and that no matter what happened in life, we could get through it together. He was everything I had ever hoped for and more. We spent every possible minute of every day together…ten minutes between classes, a quick lunch, a walk to our cars after classes, a phone call once we were home. We never wanted to be apart after that first semester and very seldom did a day go by that we didn't spend time with each other, if only for a few minutes. We counted the hours until we could see each other again. We dated exclusively for the four years of college. From the first day of our dating relationship, neither of us thought about or wanted to be with anyone else. We were married the August after our college graduation in 1992. We never doubted for a minute that we were meant to be together. We knew we had found the love of a lifetime.

The following eight years went by pretty quickly and smoothly. The first year of our marriage, neither of us had full time jobs, so things were pretty lean, but they were good. Bill was not able to find a full time job using his degree that paid much of anything and that could support the two of us, but the Lord blessed him with a good paying job in a factory working on an assembly line. It was not his dream job and not what he expected to be doing with his life, but it provided benefits and allowed us to be financially independent. He had a rough time at first accepting that he was not using his college training and adjusting to life inside of a factory, but we made it over the bumps and recognized that is where the Lord had put him. It was another example to me of how he always put his own wants aside for the good of us as a couple. I had landed a teaching job at a small Christian school so we were both now working full time, had worked our way up from living with Bill's mom, to an apartment to a condo to our own house. We traveled quite a bit and spent our free time with family and friends and enjoyed it being just the two of us. We had four nieces and nephews that we loved to visit and play with, but then it was so nice to be able to leave and have the peace and quiet of just us again. The subject of having a family and raising children rarely came up in conversation. When we were first married, of course, people would ask the routine expected question of, "When are you going to start trying to have a baby?" We would laugh and shrug it off and say we weren't ready. After several years, people just quit asking. I don't think either of us honestly thought about children when we were married or during those first blissful years. We were completely happy with life as it was, just the two of us. We didn't feel a strong desire to have children or that we needed to fill some kind of emptiness that we had. Our friends were having babies and that was great...for them. We'd go to visit the babies and do the obligatory holding, but when we left the homes of the new families, we'd sigh and think "better them than us." It never left us feeling like we wanted that or needed that. I don't think I ever made a conscience decision that I never wanted children. Growing up, I guess I imagined myself getting married and having a family just like my parents did. But it wasn't so much because I desired and deeply wanted a family. It was more because that's just what you did, it's what was expected. We were an oddity not having children right away and not planning our family for the future. I think in the back of my mind it was just something that would happen later…much later.

And so life went on, and we were content.

I don't know what it was that made me start to think about having a baby. There wasn't one particular incident or situation that made me start thinking about our future and wanting a family. It happened slowly. Part of it might have been maturity. I was getting older and that always makes you look at life a little differently. I was pushing thirty and really dreading it! Most people say turning thirty didn't bother them, but that was a rough birthday for me. I had left my teaching job for several reasons and had hung my erasers up for a while. I didn't know what to do with myself. I felt like I was a high school kid trying to decide what to do with the rest of her life. By the time someone is thirty, she is supposed to have it all figured out, or so I thought. She is supposed to have her career and family and know what direction her life is taking. I felt like a fish out of water, flopping around on dry land and gasping for every breath. So a family started to sound nice. It was a direction. Besides, I had been teaching for a few years, and I loved working with the kids and teaching them. How wonderful it would be to have my own child to teach and to show the world to.

Bill wasn't quite on board about starting a family the same time I was. We had talked about not having kids, so when I told him I wanted to have a baby I blew him completely out of the water. He did not know that I had been thinking about wanting a baby. I remember he came home from being out one day, and I was waiting for him in the living room. I told him I had been thinking and that I wanted to try to have a baby. His response, besides pure shock, was, "Okay….Not right this minute." I let him warm up to the idea and didn't push it or talk too much about it. I think he had a difficult time seeing himself as old enough and mature enough to be someone's parent. We both did, I guess. We both still felt like we were eighteen and had a hard time admitting that we were almost thirty. He was also working the second shift at work which meant he worked from four in the afternoon until one in the morning. He didn't like the idea of having a baby and then either having to work or sleep through it all. He also had some issues with his father that he had to work through. His dad was not a good dad, and their relationship had been strained over the years. I think that had something to do with his hesitation. I think he was scared that he wouldn't be a good father because he never had one to model after. I was never worried about that. He was so patient and giving and selfless; there was nothing he could be except for a wonderful father. His mother had done an amazing job of raising her son to be a respectful, caring, genuine man. I had every confidence that he would be a loving father. His schedule at work was going to change to more regular hours, and he finally realized that he was old enough-like it or not-to be a dad. He took me on a trip for my thirtieth birthday to Lake Erie. I had wanted to leave town for my birthday. If you're out of town and not home, the birthday can't find you, right? We were driving home from dinner one night while we were gone, and Bill surprised me by telling me that he was ready to have a family. He said he was going to be on day shift in a few months, and we could start trying then. I was so happy. I remember riding the rest of the way back to our bed and breakfast in silence, alone with my thoughts. I remember thinking that this could be the last vacation where it was just him and me. Life was going to be different, and I was excited about it.

We had been married for eight years and felt physically, emotionally, and financially ready. Bill had a stable job, and the place where I had been working was closing so it was perfect timing for me to get acclimated to staying at home and preparing to be a full-time mother. So in the spring of 2000, I stopped taking the birth control pill and started planning and counting days and trying to time sex just right. We expected, as many couples do, that it would happen for us right away, maybe a few months at the longest. So we began our journey of trying to create a life. It was fun and exciting, at first. After five or six months, it began to get frustrating. Every month was an intense roller coaster ride of emotions for me. At the beginning of each of my cycles, I would think, this is going to be the month. I tried to time everything perfectly, watched what I ate, took my prenatal vitamins, drank a glass of orange juice every day, walked routinely, and would convince myself we had succeeded. Every time I felt a twinge or a pain, I knew it was my body beginning to nurture a new life. I would figure what my due date would be and begin daydreaming about buying baby clothes and baby furniture. I would think of names and read Web sites where other women had posted how they knew they were pregnant. Of course, I had all of the symptoms, or so I had made myself believe. And then it would happen. I would start my period. First would come shock, then anger, then sadness, and then the tears. We hadn't been successful. Now we had to start all over again, and I would have to wait an eternity of another month to find out if I was going to be a mother. Sometimes, I wouldn't start. My periods were very unpredictable. I, again, would convince myself that I was late only because I was pregnant, so I would buy a home pregnancy test. I would take it in the morning and read all the directions and wait anxiously for the specified minutes to pass. I would hold my breath and peek at the window on the stick. There would only be one line. Sometimes I would stare at it forever, squinting and trying to make myself see two lines. "Could that be a second line? Maybe it's just faint. Maybe if I wait a few more minutes, it'll show up and get darker." But that never happened. I would end up angry at my body and throw the test away, buried under tear drenched tissues. And so the roller coaster of feeling hopeful and confident and then sad and frustrated would begin again. And so it continued.

2
HAPPY SURPRISE

So there I sat on the exam table on that Tuesday morning in May eager for the routine annual visit to the gynocologist to be over. The nurse asked her usual questions, one being when my last cycle was. I told her. I was a little late, but nothing out of the ordinary for me. My cycles had been irregular since going off my birth control medication. She asked if I wanted a pregnancy test, and I agreed knowing that once again I was going to be let down. I performed the ritual of peeing in the cup, which I had become quite a pro at over the past year. Then I waited. I can still see and hear the nurse when she came back into the exam room waving the stick with a big smile on her face and saying, "It's positive!" I didn't know what to say or what to think. I stared at her blankly. "Is it true? Am I really pregnant? I don't feel pregnant. Is this really happening?" I kept looking at the stick, and my head was trying so hard to believe and process these lines that I had been waiting so long to see. It was a doctor's office pregnancy test, so it had to be true, right? Very quickly, my mind turned to how I was going to share the news with Bill. He was going to be so happy! My mind was racing with excitement, and I was eager to share my news. I had to come back down from my cloud for a few minutes and finish the exam. The nurse figured my due date to be January 4, 2002. The holidays were going to be so much fun!

The doctor came in and congratulated me. Wow! It felt so good to finally know that I was pregnant. All of those months of planning and preparation had finally paid off. This was it!

During my exam, the doctor felt a cyst on my ovary. He asked if I had any pain, and I said no. He told me it shouldn't be a problem during my pregnancy, but that he would keep an eye on it. He wanted me to have an ultrasound done the following week so he could see exactly where it was and how large it was. So we scheduled that appointment, and I scurried off with my head back in the clouds to try to think of a way to tell Bill that he was finally going to be a father. It was a sunny, glorious day. The sky was blue, the birds were singing, and there was no one on earth happier than me. I remember getting in my car and thanking God for this gift and asking Him to keep me and the baby healthy. Our dream had finally come true!

One thing that I hadn't really put much thought into was how I was going to tell Bill when it finally happened. I had been so focused on getting pregnant that I hadn't taken any time to stop and dream about that moment when I told him he was going to be a father. You only get one first time to tell your husband that you are going to be parents. I knew I wanted it to be special, and I knew I wanted to tell him face to face, but I also knew that I wasn't going to be able to keep it from him for more than a few seconds. I still had several hours to wait until he was home from work, and that was going to take all of my patience. I stopped by a local department store and just bought a pair of baby booties. It felt strange being in the baby aisle. I was really buying something for our baby. I wanted to shout to everyone in the store, "These are for my baby! I'm finally pregnant!" I could hardly contain myself and I probably looked goofy going about the store with a silly grin. I just couldn't stop smiling.

When Bill finally got home, I met him in the garage. The day seemed to have lasted an eternity! The minutes just drug on and on and on. I was obsessed with the clock and counting how much longer until he got home from work. I started watching for his truck a good half hour before I expected him home, fantasizing that by watching the street I could magically make him appear and I wouldn't have to bust. I hurried into the garage when I saw his little pick up truck pull into the driveway. He asked how my appointment had gone, and I said fine. He did not expect anything because I had not expected anything. Then I brought the booties out from behind my back and just held them in my hands so he could see them. He looked at me a little puzzled, and then it hit him. His eyes grew big and he said, "Are you pregnant?" I grinned from ear to ear and said, "You're going to be a daddy!" We hugged and then just stood there in the garage looking at each other still trying to soak it in, trying to wrap our brains around the idea. We spent the next day or so in shock. Was this really true? Were we really going to be parents? It seemed like a dream.

No one in our family knew that we were trying to get pregnant except for my sister. She knew that we had been talking about it, but I'm not even sure that she knew we were actively trying. This wasn't the kind of news we wanted to share over the phone; we had to do it face to face. Mother's Day was in just a few days. What a perfect time to share our news! It would be just like in the movies…..the big unexpected glorious announcement.

My doctor's appointment was on a Tuesday, and we weren't planning on going to my parents house until Saturday. What a long four days! It was so hard to talk to our family on the phone and not tell them. We were about to burst with anticipation of how surprised and happy they were going to be! Our heads were swimming with all of the initial thoughts and plans of expectant parents… possible names for the baby, a theme for the nursery, baby furniture we needed. It was difficult to concentrate or focus on anything else. I was surprised at how quickly I fell in love with our baby and felt bonded to him. From the moment the nurse had said "it's positive," I felt protective of this tiny baby. I instantly loved this innocent, precious life we had created and wanted to do everything I possibly could to nurture him and keep him safe.

Saturday finally came. We were at my parent's house. We tried to play it cool and talked casually for a while, but we couldn't wait any longer! It took a few moments for it to sink in to my parents what we were telling them. They had four grandchildren already, thanks to my very fertile sister, and had probably given up on us blessing them with any more. When we asked them how they would feel about being grandparents again, they just looked at us and asked if we were getting another dog. We had a basset hound at the time who was very much spoiled and our baby. When we didn't say anything in response, my mom finally realized we were talking about a human baby. Her eyes got very big and her jaw dropped to the floor and she shouted, "You're pregnant!" We nodded and hugged and, of course, cried. My dad just kept grinning. They were both very surprised, but very happy. Oh, how I had dreamed of this day over the past year! We had wanted to knock them off their feet, and we succeeded! We had a few minutes to share together before my sister's family arrived to celebrate Mother's Day. I will never forget the expressions on my parent's faces that day.

My sister hadn't been there long until I took her off to a bedroom to tell her our news in private. I wanted it to be a sister moment. I simply asked her if she still had her crib. She knew right away and was very surprised, as well. We hugged and cried. I was so thankful to have her and my mom to help me and guide me through pregnancy and being a mother. Our nieces and nephews who were thirteen, ten, eight, and five, were gathered in the living room waiting for dessert. Bill and I told them we had a question to ask them before we ate. They had no idea. We asked what they thought about having a new baby cousin. Our niece who was thirteen knew right away what we were saying and jumped up to give us a hug. The others caught on and followed. It was wonderful night filled with excitement and joy and anticipation of the addition of a new member to our family. We were floating above the clouds.

The next day was Mother's Day, so we went to visit Bill's mom. She, too, had no idea at all that we had been planning to have a family. Both she and my parents had been great about not butting in when it came to family planning. We knew, of course, that they would be happy for us when and if we decided to have a baby, but they never asked questions or dropped little hints about when we were going to start trying to get pregnant. We had been married now for nine years, so the thought probably didn't enter their minds too often anymore. Bill and I appreciated and respected them for that. We simply signed her Mother's Day card "Love, Bill, Sandy, and Baby Hickman." She just starred at the card for a little longer than usual and then turned to us with a puzzled look. We smiled and nodded and then she understood what we were telling her. She was very excited and happy once the shock had worn off. This was going to be her first grandchild.

We really enjoyed the next week or so of surprising our friends with our news and window shopping for baby clothes and furniture. We began painting the nursery and bought the crib bedding and a few other little things. It was really beginning to sink in that we were going to have a baby. Each day, I fell more in love with the idea of being a mommy and with our precious baby. My doctor did an ultrasound at six weeks so that he could see the cyst that he had felt during my exam. The cyst was a little large, but again, he wasn't concerned about it causing problems during the pregnancy. I was able to see and hear the baby's heartbeat that day. That was amazing! I wish Bill could've been there. I really didn't feel pregnant, but I could certainly see the tiny heart beating so strong. It was a bit of a surreal moment to see it on the screen and know that a human life was growing and forming inside of me. Even though I hadn't felt pregnant, I saw the heartbeat on the screen. I really was! I remember calling my family and telling them I really was pregnant! We had been blessed to have partnered with God to create this wonderful and amazing life. Life was good, and we were eagerly awaiting the day when we would be able to hold this precious gift and see the face of our beautiful child. Then it happened.

3
MY NIGHTMARE BEGINS

Not long after the ultrasound, I experienced a little bit of spotting- not much, but enough to concern me. I called a good friend of mine who had already been through a pregnancy and explained everything to her. She reassured me that it is normal to have some minimal spotting, but that if it happened again, I should call my doctor just to be sure. I tried to rationalize it, but something in my gut just told me that something was wrong. I knew things were going to get worse. I did call my doctor a few days later because it had happened again. I spoke with his nurse, and she, too, said it was normal and that I should drink plenty of fluids and put my feet up when I could and take it easy. That was it? Didn't the doctor want to see me? Wasn't he as afraid as I was? Shouldn't somebody be more concerned? I did as I was told and tried with great effort to not let my mind go to the place I feared. I tried to pretend that everything was normal and went about the business of trying to prepare for a baby. But I was so scared on the inside! Every trip to the bathroom was a dreaded experience, waiting and holding my breath to see if I was bleeding any more. I became obsessed with checking every hour or sometimes even more frequently. I wanted to know, but I didn't want to know. I researched spotting during early pregnancy in my pregnancy books and on different web sites and again tried to rationalize that everything was going to be alright, even though I knew it wasn't. I tried not to talk about it because saying it out loud would mean it was real. So I kept my fears to myself and suffered alone. This was the first lesson in the class of "pretending to be okay to everyone when you're really not." Of course Bill knew what was going on, but I did not allow him to know the measure of my fear and certainty that something was wrong. I believe it was a coping mechanism of still trying to pretend it wasn't happening, of sticking my head in the sand. This went on for several weeks. I finally called the doctor again one Friday afternoon because the bleeding had become more frequent. He made arrangements for me to come into the office first thing Saturday morning so that he could do another ultrasound to see what was happening. I was directing our church's Vacation Bible School that year and the kick-off was to be Saturday. I knew I needed to let someone know that I was not going to be there and possibly not be able to be there for the week. So I took care of business and made my phone call and sat down and cried.

That night we went to dinner with some friends. It was a long night. I was not in any mood to socialize, but I thought it would help take my mind off things for a while. I was wrong. I managed to get through the meal and was glad to be able to go home where I could be by myself and just be me, no pretending. We went to bed soon after we got home. Bill had to be at work at 6:00 the next morning, and I was ready to go to sleep to try to escape my reality. That's when the bleeding became heavier. And then came the cramps. I know I must've gone to the bathroom at least every ten minutes or so. Bill is a very sound sleeper, so he had no idea how frequently I was getting out of bed or what was going on. I knew he had to go to work the next day, so I didn't want to wake him. Besides, what could he do? Looking back, I wish I had woke him and not suffered by myself. The cramping was horrible, but the emotional pain of knowing what was happening made them almost unbearable. I knew I was losing our baby. So for the better part of the night, I kept to myself and cried and tried to come to terms with the idea of having a miscarriage. I still hate to say that word, even more than ten years later. It's such an ugly and horrible word. I finally woke Bill around 3:00am and told him what was happening. I wanted him to call my doctor because the pain was so intense. I was scared. The doctor said there was nothing we could do. If that's what was happening, nature had to do it's job. He said I could take something for the pain, but what kind of medicine heals the pain of a broken heart? I didn't sleep at all that night.

Bill went on to work that morning because it was difficult to get excused for a Saturday. It was easier to go in and leave early. He left work early and picked me up for the ultrasound appointment. I was very quiet. The bleeding and the cramps had stopped for the most part. I was certain of what the ultrasound was going to show, but Bill stayed optimistic during the short ride to the office.

He hadn't seen and felt what I had seen and felt during the night. It was a Saturday, so there weren't many people in the office which was a good thing. The nurse who does the ultrasounds called us back and began the procedure. I held Bill's hand and kept starring at the screen trying to see that tiny heartbeat I had just seen a few weeks before and holding on to the hope that maybe Bill was right. It took an eternity. The nurse never spoke a word. Her face spoke volumes. I knew she was searching everywhere she knew to search for our baby. But it was gone.

She told me to get dressed and to wait in the exam room for the doctor. He confirmed our fears. I had miscarried. He said the baby probably died not long after my first ultrasound and it took my body several weeks to discard the tissue. He said he wanted to do a D & C to be sure all of the tissue was gone. He also said that the cyst he had found on my ovary needed to be removed before it became any larger or caused any other problems, especially if I wanted to try to get pregnant again. Bill and I agreed, and the doctor said he would try to schedule it for Monday. It would require an incision and an overnight stay in the hospital. I certainly didn't want to have surgery, but I welcomed the distraction no matter what it was. I couldn't think too much about the fact that I had lost the pregnancy...I needed to focus on me having surgery and preparing things around the house for me to be out of commission for a while. There were groceries to buy and laundry to do and bills to pay. I didn't have time to think about what had just happened. That was good, right?

When Bill and I arrived home after that awful appointment, we knew we had to make a few phone calls letting people know what had happened and that I was scheduled for surgery. I was an absolute mess and knew that I wouldn't be able to handle telling our family and close friends. I didn't want to have to say the words "miscarriage" or "lost the baby." I just couldn't make myself utter them out loud. So Bill, who was also dealing with a lot of emotions, took to the task of making the necessary calls. He has a gift for being able to hold it together to get done what needs to be done. He called our family to tell them the news. Of course, they already knew what had been going on and what I had suspected. It just needed to be confirmed. I'm sure my parents offered to do anything for us and asked what we needed, but they did not come to the house over the weekend. Looking back, it must have been so difficult for them to stay away. I'm sure they wanted to hug us and "do" something for us. They were hurting too. They hurt because they had lost a grandchild and because they knew we were hurting. But all Bill and I wanted was each other. We didn't want to think about what happened or talk about it. We just wanted to go to bed and try to sleep to escape this horrible reality that had slammed into us. And so we did.

I don't remember much else about that weekend. I do remember going to the grocery store on Sunday to stock up for the next few weeks and trying to pretend that I was okay. I was trying to fool my head into thinking only about the surgery and not about any of that other unpleasantness. I guess I ate. I guess I bathed. I guess I breathed.

My surgery was on Monday, June 9 in the afternoon. One month and one day after I had found out I was pregnant and had been soaring in the clouds. Bill went in to work that morning to take care of the paperwork that needed to be filled out in order for him to take the week off. I busied myself with last minute preparations and packing an overnight bag. If I kept busy, I wouldn't have to think about it. I had never had surgery as an adult. I was very scared. I had no idea what to expect before or after. The nurses at the hospital were wonderful. They could probably tell I was nervous. I'm not sure if they were aware that I had just lost a baby. No one spoke of it. They were very good about telling me what was happening and patient with my many questions. I asked Bill to stay with me every possible second that he could, but I didn't have to ask. He was always there. He knew I was scared and nervous. He was nervous too, but he never let me know. He stayed right by my side up until they wheeled me to the operating room. My parents and my sister came to the hospital, and they gave us a hug. I could see the love and tenderness and the sorrow in their eyes, but I held back my tears. I was afraid if I started to cry, I wouldn't be able to stop. I put on my brave and "I'm not worried" face and spent time trying to comfort and reassure everybody else. I don't remember anyone talking about the pregnancy loss. I was trying to keep it buried and they probably weren't sure what to say or if I wanted to talk about it. So we kept the conversation on the lighter side and focused on the surgery and all the activity that was going on in preparation. I kept my reality of the miscarriage at arm's length. It was too nasty and difficult to deal with. So I ignored it.

The surgery went fine, but the doctor had to remove one ovary and fallopian tube because the cyst had grown into and around them. He said it was not a problem to just have one ovary and tube and that I should be able to get pregnant again. He didn't see an obvious reason for the miscarriage. The cyst had nothing to do with it. It was probably an unhealthy embryo. One in four pregnancies ends in miscarriage, a statistic that I had never heard or dreamed of. Apparently they are very common. Most women go on to have healthy pregnancies. The medical world does not raise an eyebrow unless a woman has three consecutive miscarriages. Well, I didn't have to worry about that. That was not going to be me.

Physically, after my surgery, it was rough. I had no idea how much pain I would be in. The surgery required a bikini line incision. The first night, I stayed in the hospital, and Bill stayed with me. I couldn't even imagine him not being with me, for emotional support and to give me comfort. I began to feel very clingy towards him. I didn't want to be away from him for even one second. I had never stayed overnight in a hospital before. I remember I could not turn over in bed because of the pain. Even just turning a little from side to side was difficult, and I had to use the bed rails. Bill was there during the night to help me or move a pillow or get me ice. As long as I didn't move, I was okay.

The next morning, the nurse came in to help me up out of bed for the first time. Oh! The pain! It hurt so bad I thought I was going to cry. I couldn't stand up straight, and I had to take little tiny steps. Just sitting down to go to the restroom was a major event. They sent me home that afternoon. My sister, Patti, and my thirteen year old niece, Katie, came to the house with us and helped me get settled. Bill went straight to bed. He had tried to sleep sitting up in a chair all night at the hospital, in between taking care of me. He was emotionally and physically exhausted. My sister decided to stay the night so she could help me and Bill could get some rest. I was so glad that she did! I hardly slept. Every time I moved, I thought my incision was ripping open and I felt every single muscle in my stomach. Patti was always right there when I needed her and helped me go to the restroom and kept me up to date on my medicines. It was a very long night. She and my niece left the next morning, a Wednesday. Bill had until Monday off work, and he was rested. I stayed in bed for the next few days and limited my use of the stairs. I really missed the rails on the hospital bed! I didn't have anything to pull on to help me turn over. Bill got to the point of raising his arm for me to pull on and not even waking up. I wasn't able to stand up straight for about two weeks. I had not anticipated my body taking that long to heal. Bill, Patti, and my mom were all great with helping to take care of the house, the dog, and all of the chores and errands. I was really surprised at how long it took for me to feel back to normal in a physical sense. It was almost six months before I could be active and not be aware of those stomach muscles.

Emotionally, I was a wreck, but not willing to admit it. The surgery, my physical needs, and healing pushed my emotions and grief to the background. That was a nice place to keep them, so I continued to keep them there. If I kept pushing them back, I wouldn't have to confront them and deal with the hurt and the pain and the grief. It was much easier. So I thought. I began playing the game of trying to make everyone else feel better about the situation. "I'm fine, I'm doing okay, and I'll be alright," became my standard answers followed by a change of subject when anyone asked how I was doing. I became very good at putting on a smile and acting as though I was handling the situation with ease. I must have been pretty good because I think everyone bought it, even myself. If you lie about something often enough, it tends to become a reality to you. I had fooled myself into thinking I was okay and didn't need any help or anyone. I was just fine on my own.

Bill and I went away for our anniversary in August to Niagara Falls. It was about two months after the miscarriage and my surgery. We drove and stopped at places we wanted to visit along the way. We stopped at Lake Erie which was beautiful. It was our first time visiting one of the Great Lakes when it wasn't frozen. We strolled along the beach and saw a lighthouse, which is one of our hobbies. We stayed at Niagara Falls for several days and drove quite a bit enjoying the scenery of New York and several more lighthouses. It was very low key and laid back. It was a fun trip, and I really enjoyed our time spent together alone. I expected things were getting back to normal and that I had succeeded in not having to deal with any grief. I had outsmarted it and found a loophole. I had bypassed the ugliness and we'd just try again to get pregnant and that would be that. But it wasn't that simple.

The grief and pain kept pushing its way to the surface. I would push it back down, but it kept getting stronger and more frequent and more persistent. I wasn't able to hold it off. It was making me weak trying to fight it. It was a constant battle.

Nighttime was the worst. The house would be quiet and my thoughts had all the time in the world to get carried away. It was so lonely. During the day, I expected to feel lonely because I was at home by myself. At night, Bill was home. I didn't expect to feel lonely. But I did. He has been blessed with the ability to fall asleep as soon as his head hits the pillow and to sleep fairly sound. So he would drift off to sleep, and I would lie there next to him feeling so alone. I would cry myself to sleep most every night. He had no idea how much I was hurting or how alone I felt because I did not tell him. I was still trying so hard to keep up the façade of being a strong person and being able to handle the grips of devastation. Losing the baby was sad for Bill, but it had not stopped his world like it had mine. He was hopeful that we would try again and that we would be successful. I couldn't even dream of moving on. It wouldn't be fair to our baby! How could we just forget and try again?

The guilt, at times, was overwhelming. I felt guilty for so many things. I hadn't been able to protect our helpless little baby. I had tried with all I had, but failed. I felt guilty for not being able to provide my husband with the child he wanted. I felt guilty for not having a body that could do what God had designed it to do. I felt guilty for feeling guilty.

As fall and the thought of the holidays approached, I could feel the grief and pain that I had been suppressing pushing its way to the surface harder and harder. It was a battle every day to keep those pesky unpleasant emotions out of the way. I remember days of staying in bed until almost time for Bill to get home from work. Then I would hop up and take a shower and scurry about the house doing the basic chores so that he would think all was well. When he got home, I glued my happy face back on and began my act. I slept a lot. A phrase from a Carly Simon song comes to mind, "I stayed in bed all morning just to pass the time…" It was the only way of keeping my thoughts and feelings out of the way. It was the only way I knew to cope.

I had quit my job, and I wasn't working, so I had no reason to get out of bed in the morning. If it hadn't been for our dog needing to go outside and needing to eat, I probably wouldn't even have gone downstairs. I don't remember my social life too much at that point. I guess I did things with my friends and family because no one caught on to my act, but I don't remember. I do remember just going through the motions at Thanksgiving and Christmas. It had become a tradition in our family over the past few years to have Thanksgiving at our house, so this year wasn't about to be any different. I wasn't going to do anything that would alert my family that I wasn't fine and dandy. Everything had to go on as usual. Then I would not have to admit that I wasn't okay and not up to the festivities. Typically, I think Thanksgiving can be a rather boring holiday. It's all about the food. We spend all day preparing the yummy dishes and in less than half an hour, it's devoured and everyone feels miserable. Then there are all the dirty dishes to do. And, of course, there are the pies to gorge on. It's quite exhausting. So I usually try to have some kind of activity or game to help make the day be about more than the turkey. We also have four nieces and nephews, and I always want them to have a fun time at our house and not just sit around and be bored. So besides planning and shopping for the meal and cleaning the house, I had to think of something fun for us to do. It was really getting difficult to keep those emotions tucked away where I liked them to be.

I set my mind to the task of preparing for the day and making it the best Thanksgiving ever. I felt the need to go above and beyond what I would normally do just to prove how well I was doing and show everyone how strong and capable I was. I pulled it off. I managed to make it through the day with my smile and my "I'm so thankful" attitude. I managed to pull off a fabulous meal and a few fun games. The table decorations were cute and each place setting had a little candle and favor. We had a meaningful time of sharing what we were thankful for. I had to fight back the tears so hard. It was a Thanksgiving to remember, but

I couldn't wait for everyone to leave. I wanted to retreat to my bed which had become my faithful friend, always there, where I didn't have to pretend anymore and I could let the tears that were struggling so much to come finally flow. I was miserable.

Christmas was much the same, only drawn out for a whole month. I did finally admit to Bill that I didn't have any Christmas spirit. I had no desire or interest to decorate a tree, make cookies, sing carols, go to parties, buy gifts, or participate in anything jolly. Christmas is his favorite time of year. He starts counting the number of days until Christmas on December 26. He loves the decorations, all of the cookies and candies, the parties, the songs, buying and wrapping gifts, all of the things that I wanted to ignore. I usually loved these things too. But this year, it was different. I was supposed to be nine months pregnant. We were supposed to be getting close to having a baby and imagining what the next Christmas would be like with a baby that was almost one year old. This was supposed to be the last Christmas with just two stockings hung over the fireplace. The next Christmas we were supposed to be able to buy our baby gifts and hang "Baby's First Christmas" ornaments on the tree. I was supposed to be big and round like Santa and not able to shop because of my pregnant, tired body. It was supposed to be a holiday filled with excitement and anticipation. Instead, it was empty and sad. I muddled through, though I truly don't remember too much about Christmas that year. I look back at pictures of the family on Christmas Eve and see us all together so I know it happened, but I have no memory of it. I guess I put myself on autopilot to be able to get through it all. I love our nieces and nephews dearly, but I really was dreading watching them open their gifts and talking about Santa. Christmas is a very child oriented holiday and I wanted no part of it. I just remember being sad when the entire rest of the world was happy and singing. It reminded me of the song <u>River</u> by Joni Mitchell that talked about wishing for a river to skate away on to escape singing songs and taking part in the festivities of Christmas. I so wished for a river!

As my due date of January 4 drew closer, I began to lose the battle with my emotions buried deep. They were pushing up harder than I could push them down. After Bill went to bed on the night of January 3rd, I sat by myself for a long while just thinking and crying. Thinking of what should have been and the happiness I should have been feeling. I felt I needed to do something to commemorate the day of my due date. I felt like something needed to be done to remember the precious baby that we never were able to see or hold. A life had been lost, but there had been no funeral or memorial service. There had not been anything done to record or to remember my precious baby. There had never been any closure, and I needed something. I had read of people writing letters to their loved ones who had died as a way of saying good-bye, so that's what I decided to do. At least it was something. It wasn't a long letter, but a letter telling our baby how special he was, how long we had wanted him, how much I loved him, that I would see him in Heaven some day, and how I would never forget him. It was a healing and powerful way of saying goodbye. I placed the letter in a shoebox along with the ultrasound picture and all of the cards people had sent to us and closed the lid and placed it on a shelf in the basement. I finally felt as if I had buried our baby and could move forward.

My mom came to the house the next day. She had remembered my due date, and I was thankful for her. We went to lunch and I shared a little about how I had been feeling. I don't think she knew much to say. She had never experienced a pregnancy loss. But it meant so much to know that she remembered and cared. Bill brought me home a bouquet of flowers. I still remember how beautiful they were and how touched I was. He is an amazing man.

We had started painting the room that was to be the nursery after we found out I was pregnant. I had gone to visit a friend from college not long after that first doctor visit. She was so excited for us! She already had two children and loaded my car up with baby things. She loaned me her bassinet, some maternity clothes, and other odds and ends. We had spent the weekend talking about pregnancy things and baby things. After I returned home, Bill and I went shopping and bought the crib bedding and a few other little items. That hadn't been the purpose of our shopping, we were just going to look. But I found a crib bedding pattern that I loved, and I didn't want to take the chance of it being gone when I came back. We were so excited! So, we bought it. Several people gave us baby outfits they had bought and, of course, our heads were spinning thinking of all we needed to do and buy.

It was fun planning the nursery. We didn't want to find out the sex of the baby, so it had to be something neutral. We wanted to keep it simple, but cute. And then the world turned upside down. We closed the door to the nursery and kept it closed. It was at the end of the hall, so I didn't have to walk by it very often, which was good. I did muster up the strength to return the bedding we had bought when spring came. Always the practical one, I didn't want to wait too long and then not be able to return it. Besides, it held bad memories. If I did get pregnant again, I wanted it to be new and fresh. So, one day I very quickly opened the nursery door, grabbed the huge bag and headed to the department store. I had to leave my emotions at home and just think very matter-of-factly. I couldn't think about what I was doing; I just needed to do it. So I set my mind to the task at hand. I did okay. The lady working at the return desk had me fill out my name, etc. and there in what seemed like gigantic bold print was the question "reason for return." I simply put "no longer needed." She gave me my money and out the door I headed. I sat down in the car, put the key in the ignition, and bawled. I had held it together just long enough.

Spiritually, I was trying to be a super Christian. You know what that means, right? I did not want to admit to anyone, most of all myself, that I didn't understand God's plan, that I was angry with God, or that I felt He was being unfair. I was trying to hold it all together and put on the façade of handling the situation. I was pretending to have a super strong faith to impress God and others. I had been raised in the church, came from Christian parents, and had been a Christian myself since I was a child. Intellectually, I knew all the answers; emotionally and spiritually I was struggling. This was the first time I had ever felt disappointed with God and unsure of His plans and reasons for allowing things to happen. My faith was being tried. During this time, I never questioned the existence of God and was never tempted to turn my back on Him. I just didn't understand why He had allowed this to happen to me. He was God. He created the entire universe and everything that has ever been in existence, so He certainly could've saved our baby and let him live. So why didn't He? What had I done wrong that He would punish me this way? Was He trying to teach me a lesson? Couldn't it have been taught some other way and our baby's life spared? Why were fifteen year old girls and women addicted to heroine or alcohol allowed to have babies and me denied? I felt it was all very unfair.

We didn't attend church services for a while after the miscarriage, maybe a few months. One reason was because I was angry with God, and I certainly didn't feel like singing praises to Him. I still loved Him, I just didn't like Him right then. I needed my time to pout. Church can also be very emotional. The songs could easily evoke emotions that I wanted so desperately to keep at bay. Another reason we stayed away was a more social one. I didn't want to be around other people. I think it is difficult to be around lots of people when you are grieving. This was something I struggled with for several months after each of my pregnancy losses. It was a confusing emotion, even to me. On one hand, I wanted people to be sad with me and cry with me, and I wanted to know that they cared. On the other hand, I didn't want to talk to people about it. I didn't want to face people asking how I was doing. Maybe partly because I knew I was going to lie to them and say I was doing okay. I have found that when people, for the most part, see you on a Sunday morning and ask you how you are doing, they are just being polite. It is just a pleasantry to exchange. They want and expect you to smile and say fine and continue down the hall. They don't expect a true and honest answer. And those who would actually give me a few seconds of their time always felt they had to SAY something. I certainly didn't want to hear people telling me that it was just not meant to be, that the baby was not healthy, that there would be other babies. Did they not understand that this was MY baby they were talking about? I loved him, no matter what. He wasn't a pet hamster that I could just forget about and go get another. It was a human life, a life created by me and Bill. It was half of me and half of him. I didn't want another baby; I wanted THIS baby. It was very difficult for me to listen to people try to excuse away the pregnancy. Don't make excuses! Just say you're sorry and that you love me. That's what I needed.

I also found it difficult when people, fellow Christians, thought this was a good time to preach to me. Romans 8:28 was quoted to me many times, "And we know that all things work together for good to them that love God, to them who are the called according to His purpose." That is the word of God, and I believe it to be true. But that is not what I needed to hear at a time when my loss was still so fresh and the wounds still open and bleeding. I took offense when anyone tried to tell me that there was ANY good in what had happened to me. Looking back now, years later, I can see the good. But I believe Romans 8:28 is a verse to share after a person has gone through the trial, not while they are caught up right in the midst of it. So, I didn't want to go to church and have to be surrounded by people and pretend all was well and listen to their ignorant remarks. I know they meant well. I think grief related to death is just something that our society, even our Christian family, does not handle well. Part of the "good" that came from all of this is that I feel better equipped to minister to someone who is dealing with this kind of grief. I know she doesn't want my opinion or to hear me ramble on about God's plan. She just wants me to listen, say I'm sorry, and give her a big hug. She wants to know I care, that I took time out of my life to spend a little while in hers. She wants to know I am praying for her silently and maybe aloud with her.

I was slipping down into a deep, dark pit. I didn't realize just how deep and dark the pit was going to be.

4
PREGNANT AGAIN

A few months later in March 2002, I found out I was pregnant again. I had gone on a weekend trip with my sister and her four kids to Tennessee. I should have started my period before we left, but I hadn't. I tried to be relaxed and laid back about it. I had jumped the gun before and spent needless money on pregnancy tests, so I wanted to wait at least a few days. Besides, I wanted to know, but I didn't want to know. If the test was negative, then that meant one more wasted month of trying and we had to start all over again. If the test was positive, then that meant constant worry and stress. I tried to not think about it too much and just enjoy the time with my nieces and nephews, but every time my mind was still, that's where my thoughts turned. I don't think I shared with my sister the possibility that I thought I was pregnant. Bill knew and asked every time I called home if I had started yet. He was anxious to know.

On Monday, I was back home and went to the store first thing and bought a test. I had bought a generic brand because I was so tired of wasting money just to get a negative result. I came home and took the test. I wasn't sure if it was positive or not. I thought there were two lines, but it was very light. So I ended up back at the store and bought a brand name test anyway. That one showed two lines. No doubts or questions. I was pregnant. My emotions were mixed. I was happy. Here was another chance. All of the planning and timing had paid off. I was also afraid. The worst had happened before and it could happen again. I wasn't naïve this time. I was guarded, yet excited; anxious, yet hopeful; fearful, yet glad.

Bill was at work when I took the test. I was eager to share the news with him, but I was more calm than the first time. I patiently waited for the hours to pass trying to think of a way to tell him. It was almost like I was waiting to tell him about a great bargain I had found or a new idea I had for decorating a room, not that our lives may be about to change forever. The time almost went by too fast. When he got home, I would have to say it out loud and that would make it real.

We played a game on the computer pretty often with songs. We had a fairly large library of songs ranging from country to gospel to rock. We would play the first few seconds of a song for the other person and he or she had to guess what song it was and name the artist. We were both pretty good. That's how I decided to share the news. When Bill got home, I was upstairs where the computer was. He came up, and we said hello. I was playing things pretty cool. I asked how his day was, blah, blah, blah. And then I started playing the game. There is a song called "Arms Wide Open" by Creed. It's a song the lead singer wrote about finding out that he was going to be a father. I played the few seconds, and, of course, he guessed the song. I told him he was right and then smiled and kept looking at him. When I didn't play another song, he looked puzzled. And then he realized I was telling him something by the song I had chosen. We hugged and kissed and sat for a few minutes. We didn't say too much. We were both afraid to let our hearts be broken again. We knew something could go wrong. And it did.

We wondered if we should tell our family and friends right away or wait. We were excited, and we wanted to share the news with everyone. But we also were being realistic this time and painfully aware that it was way too early to be making plans or to be getting too excited. If we told many people, that would be the same number of people that we would have to tell the sad news to if things went wrong. But in the end, we opted to tell people. The more people who knew, the more prayers could be offered up. Besides, if something did go wrong, we would have to tell our family and friends anyway. That was something I couldn't hide. Everyone was happy for us, but they too were a bit guarded and hesitant to talk in the future tense. No one asked questions about nursery plans or names. Of course, they really didn't have much time.

The spotting was very light at first, but it was there. The first time I noticed it, my heart sank. I just sat there staring at the toilet paper. Was I really seeing it? It was so light, maybe I was imagining it. I told myself that next time it wouldn't be there. But it was. The spotting was hardly detectable it was so light, but yet it screamed volumes. It screamed "It's over!" and "You've failed again!" and "Your baby has died!" Again, I didn't want to tell anyone or speak about it at all. That would make it a reality I would have to face and deal with. I just wanted to crawl into bed and bury my head and make it all go away. I didn't want to have to go through this again. I called my doctor's office and told them about the spotting.

I received the same response as I did the first time… drink plenty of water and put my feet up when I could. I know there was really nothing else they could've told me, but it all sounded so inadequate. There was a human life, MY baby, possibly dying, and all they could do was tell me to prop my feet up. I felt so helpless. My body was completely out of my control. There was nothing, NOTHING, I could do to save my baby's life. It is the worst feeling. Part of me tried to pretend that it was going to be okay, but I knew. I knew I was miscarrying again.

I didn't go anywhere for the next week or so. I became obsessed with going to the bathroom again, hoping that one time I would go and wouldn't see any blood. Maybe the spotting was just a normal occurrence. I also wanted to do as little as possible as a valiant effort to save the life we had created and that I was now responsible for. My mom came to the house a few times and did some light cleaning, and Bill didn't allow me to carry anything. I also didn't want to be around people. It was very difficult to go out into the world and see people living their lives and their world continuing on when mine was coming to a stop. I remember one evening, my parents brought dinner over and I tried to be pleasant and talk to get my mind off of things, but it was useless. I just wanted to cry and scream. In retrospect, I wish I would have. I don't know why I thought I had to be so brave.

I had an ultrasound around six weeks. The ultrasound tech was very quiet again and I knew things were not right. The silence was extremely loud. The doctor said there should be a visible heartbeat by then, but there wasn't. He also said the sac looked smaller than it should be at six weeks. He was fairly certain that the baby had died and that I would miscarry. To be sure, he did a few blood tests. There is a hormone that is produced when you are pregnant that doubles in value every other day if everything is fine and developing normally. My levels were much lower with the second test, so the doctor knew the baby had died. He suggested doing a D&C so that I wouldn't have to go through the physical pain of miscarrying. Bill didn't want me to have to endure the pain again and neither did I. I had the procedure on April 18, exactly one month after I had found out I was pregnant.

Physically, it was a piece of cake compared to the first pregnancy loss. I was only at the hospital for a few hours and didn't have any bleeding or pain. I was thankful for being able to avoid the physical pain of the miscarriage. The first one had been almost unbearable. By the next day, I had recovered and was able to return to my normal routine, which didn't include much.

Emotionally, I was drained. I had lost two babies in less than a year, but I didn't know how to grieve. I felt I had no one to talk to who understood how I was feeling and the emotions I was trying to sort through.

I felt so alone. I was suffering miserably and silently. A few friends and acquaintances had come forward and confided in me that they also had had a miscarriage. But all of them now had children. I was grieving not only the loss of a child, but also the loss of a dream of ever being a mother. It seemed everywhere I turned there were babies and friends getting pregnant. I couldn't stand to watch television anymore. There were shows with babies, commercials with babies, shows with pregnant people, commercials for baby products and pregnancy tests. Each one was a slap in the face. When I did venture out to the grocery store or mall, I stayed as far away from the baby aisle and baby stores as I possibly could. Even when I saw a baby, I looked the other way and avoided him or her at all costs. There seemed to be no escape and no safe place to go, except for my bed. There I could drift off to sleep and escape this terrible reality that had become my life, if only for a few minutes. That was better than nothing. My identity had become lost. I was no longer Sandy. I was the woman who couldn't keep a pregnancy, the woman who had miscarried twice. That was how I saw myself. Nothing else mattered. My existence was engulfed in this truth. All of my thoughts and feelings somehow related to the losses. It was difficult to focus on anything else for any amount of time. I was consumed with pain and hopelessness. Bill was great through it all, but he did not understand all of the issues and feelings I had, the same with my family and friends. My family was wonderful if I needed the floor scrubbed or a meal cooked, but they didn't know what I was going through, either. How could they? Part of the problem was me. I didn't know how to reach out. I didn't know what I needed, so how could I let them know? I also think part of it was my family's lack of acknowledgement as to the pink elephant standing in the middle of the room screaming. It's a normal reaction, one I was just as guilty of at times. Don't mention it or talk about it, and it will all be okay. I knew they loved me and wanted my pain to go away. They just didn't know how to help. I needed someone who did.

Easter was a nightmare for me that year. It was tradition that my family got together after Sunday service for a big, delicious ham dinner at my parents' home. This year would not be any different. It had only been a few weeks since the miscarriage, but I was back at being a pro of plastering on my smile and pretending I was strong and doing just fine. I thought I could handle the afternoon out. I gave myself too much credit. I muddled through the meal without much incident. I was fairly quiet, but I guess everyone expected that. I wanted so badly to just leave and go home, but I didn't want to disappoint everyone or ruin Easter Sunday for Bill or our nieces and nephews. I was concerned about the feelings of everyone else and not paying attention to what I needed. Of course, everyone would've understood, but it was my head versus my heart. I was so miserable. I was angry for my family not talking about the loss and how I was feeling. I wanted to scream as loud as I could, "Don't you care? Don't you see how much I'm hurting and know how hard it is to face the world?" I was angry at them for going about life and for talking and laughing and eating and enjoying themselves. I was angry for them not curling up in a fetal position with me and throwing in the towel and crying until there were no more tears to cry. I had so many things I wanted to say, and yet I couldn't bring myself to say anything. I could only sit, paralyzed with all of my feelings and emotions and suffer silently. After dinner, our oldest niece and nephew sang a song for all of us that they had been working on. They both are very talented and have wonderful voices. They sang in the school show choirs and also sang specials for their church. I don't remember the song they sang that day. But I can still very vividly remember sitting in the living room at the top of the steps on the floor listening to them sing so beautifully and my heart aching and breaking. I fought back the tears with every ounce of strength I had. Their sweet voices had summoned tears of grief and sorrow and pain. I longed for the day when I could sit and watch my children and beam with the pride that my sister was showing for her children. I longed for a family of my own. I was so proud of them and thankful that they were using their talent to glorify God, but I was also grieving the family that I thought I was never going to be blessed with. I needed to go home. I needed to be able to be myself with all of my pain without the masquerade. I found comfort once again in the arms of my safe and reliable bed.

At the hospital when I had the D&C, the nurse gave me a pamphlet about a support group for men and women who had lost babies through miscarriage, stillborn birth or death soon after birth. I never considered myself a support grouper. I always thought people who went to support groups just enjoyed talking about themselves a little too much. How much good could it really do? The thought of talking in front of complete strangers was not an idea I enjoyed. But I was at the end of my rope. I knew I needed to do something. I was falling deeper and deeper into a pit with no idea of how to get out. I needed someone who had been in the pit before me to help me find a way out.

What a blessing! The support group met only once a month, but their next meeting happened to fall only a week or so after the D&C. I made the decision to go. Bill offered to go with me, but I wanted to go alone. I felt I could be more honest and open and not hold anything back, including tears, if I didn't know anyone. I've never found it easy to cry in front of people, even my husband. That has changed.

I didn't know what to expect the first time. I just wanted to go and see with my own eyes that there were other women in the world who had been through the same thing. I really didn't plan on talking too much- just listening. The group met at a local church, but there was no religious affiliation with the group. The mood was pretty somber. No one talked much while people were arriving. I walked in and found a seat relatively close to the door, so I could leave, of course, if I found the group to be too lame or too threatening. The leader was a nurse and grief counselor at a local hospital. She had a very gentle and compassionate spirit. She began our meeting by laying a few ground rules, mostly about the do's and don'ts of the meeting. One thing she said has always stuck with me. She said we were not allowed to compare circumstances--"My experience was worse or hurt more than yours." She said simply grief was grief.

That is so very true. Then, we started going around the circle, one by one, sharing our stories of what had brought us to this place. We didn't have to share if we didn't want to, but everyone did. Even me. It was so freeing to be able to talk about my feelings and have people know EXACTLY what I meant and what I was going through. It also helped to hear other people's stories--to know that I wasn't the only one this had ever happened to, that other people had suffered heartbreaks too and lived to tell about it, to hear someone put into words the way I had been feeling, but didn't know how to express it. We were all strangers, yet all connected by this bond of experiencing overwhelming joy followed by overwhelming sorrow. We were all broken and looking for someone to help us hold together. Some of us had lost our pregnancies early, like me. Some of us had lost our pregnancies in the second or third trimester. And some of us had actually given birth and been able to see the face of their precious child. But there was no desire to compare situations. Grief was grief.

The hour and a half flew by. I wished we could've just gone on sharing with each other. I didn't want it to end. I was a confirmed support grouper! When I left the church that night, I felt different. The tears I had held back for so long came unexpectedly and uncontrollably. God gave us the gift of tears to allow us a way of releasing our emotions. It is an awesome gift. I have since allowed myself to enjoy the benefit and the cleansing that tears bring. I do not feel silly anymore when tears come, nor do I feel like I need to explain or justify them. You feel what you feel. I had learned to be honest.

I began trying to find books that had been written by women who had suffered pregnancy loss. I didn't find many, but I did find a few. They were helpful to me. At least I began to feel like I wasn't completely and totally alone anymore. I felt connected, even if it was by just a single thread, to other women in the world who had gone through what I was going through.

I decided to volunteer at the community hospital where I had my surgery. I needed something to focus on besides myself. It was a blessing. For at least a few hours a week, I could forget about me and my world and help someone else. I worked in the front lobby of the hospital at the information desk. My job was to give visitors the room numbers of the patients they were visiting, give directions, answer questions, and simply make those who entered the front doors feel welcome. I did well. I enjoyed meeting people and talking with them. I especially enjoyed talking with the older folks. Sometimes they were at the hospital for some sort of test and I could tell they were scared or maybe lonely. So I'd chat with them and listen to their story or whatever else they wanted to share. It seemed to make their day just by having someone to listen to them and having someone show in an interest. My shift was only four hours a week, but I did look forward to that time. It gave me purpose and allowed me to help others. There, I was just Sandy the volunteer. The people that came through the front doors didn't know my story. They didn't know my pain, and I didn't have to pretend with them. I couldn't feel bad when they didn't ask how I was doing; that wasn't their role in the relationship. I also didn't have to worry about them trying to make me feel better or preach to me. For those four hours, I could leave my new found identity and all of my baggage at the door. Unfortunately, they were right there when I walked out of the door, and they would jump right back onto me with their stickiness and ugliness.

Spiritually, I was very confused and angry. Why wasn't God listening to my prayers? Had I not prayed enough? Why wasn't He granting me the desires of my heart? Why was He making me suffer so much? Had He turned his ear away from me? I had so many questions, but for some reason, I could not bring myself to go to anyone for answers. I don't know why. Maybe it was pride, admitting I didn't know all the answers. Maybe it was fear of talking to someone. Maybe it was the fear that they weren't going to tell me what I wanted to hear. I do remember asking my dad at some point during my journey into the pit, "Why did God allow this to happen to me?" His answer was that we are all subject to the laws of nature and that bad things will and do happen to us. We have imperfect physical bodies that do not always function and perform as they should. His answer did not satisfy me. I knew our bodies were imperfect, but I also knew that God had created the universe and everything that has ever existed and if He wanted me to have a healthy pregnancy, He could certainly make it happen. Nothing was too big or impossible for Him. I really struggled with what the difference was between God's will and the fact of that's just how we're made. It seemed to be a matter of convenience which answer to give. Some would tell me it was just the result of having an imperfect body and things do not always work the way they should, and others would tell me it was God's will and that He had a plan for me. Well, which one was it? I was very confused. Was my not being able to have a child God's will or just a matter of happenstance? I remember one day I was in the basement doing laundry and, for no apparent reason, I was overcome with grief. I just began crying uncontrollably. I still do not know what triggered it. Sometimes I didn't need a trigger. It just happened. I remember getting on my knees in front of the washer and dryer and just crying out to God, "Why aren't You listening to me? Why aren't You answering my prayers? What have I done to be forgotten like this? Why do You keep dangling the carrot in front of me and then ripping it away when I get a nibble?"

My brain and my heart battled constantly. My brain knew that God wasn't sitting in Heaven looking around for someone to pick on to make their life miserable, but my heart wasn't so sure.

"O God, do not keep silent; be not quiet, O God, be not still." Psalm 83:1

Bill was trying to understand how I was feeling. He knew I was struggling and that I was having trouble coping with my grief, but he did not know all of the many feelings I had pushing me down and destroying my self image. One day, I decided to try to write down a few of the feelings for him so that he could begin to see the enormity of my struggle. I titled it "My Baggage," and handed it to him. He wasn't expecting it, but he was glad I had given it to him. He had no idea of the battle going on inside my head and heart. He didn't really know what to do with the information, but at least he knew some of how I was feeling. I think it just solidified to him that I needed help. Here is the list of my baggage.

Anger-- I feel anger towards God, my body, the world for still spinning, people for not understanding me and going on with their lives. I am angry towards people saying it is God's plan, that everything works for good, angry for people making excuses as to why it happened.

Resentment--I resent pregnant women, women who have babies.

Frustration--I am completely frustrated for not knowing a reason for the losses and with my body not working right. I am frustrated with the doctors for not doing more.

Guilt--Did I do something to cause the miscarriages? I feel guilty when a pregnancy ends because I don't have to worry anymore. I feel guilty for letting Bill and the baby down.

Relief--I feel a sense of relief when the pregnancy ends because I no longer have to worry every second if it will be successful. The decision has been made. Then I feel guilty for feeling relieved.

Alone--I feel very alone. No one understands how I feel. People seem to forget after the first few initial days.

Confused--How am I supposed to be feeling? What's going to happen next? Should we try again? I have good days and bad days. I never know which kind of day I am going to have. I never know when I will burst into tears or when something will reopen my wounds.

Fear--Will I ever be a mom? Will Bill still love me? Do I want to risk another pregnancy?

Emptiness--I want to be pregnant. I miss knowing that there is a baby inside of me. My womb is empty.

Annoyed--It annoys me when people compare me to others and their situations.

Helplessness--There is nothing I can do to protect my babies and save them.

Restless--Sometimes I just want to scream and punch and run!

Betrayed--I feel betrayed by my body, by God. Why is it so easy for every other woman to have a baby? Why is God allowing the crack addict or the thirteen-year- old to have a baby and not me?

Heartbroken--My hopes and dreams have been ripped away. I grieve for my babies and for the family I may never have.

Bitterness-I have a lot of bitterness, mostly toward other women who can bear children.

I was feeling really down and blue one particular day and just couldn't face being at home all alone all day. I called a good friend from church who was a close friend and whom I admired for her spiritual walk. I called her and asked if I could come to her house. I just needed a friend. Of course she said to come on over. I drove the forty-five minutes through the tears, not sure exactly what I wanted or needed from her. I just knew I needed to talk to someone. She greeted me with open arms and a huge hug. She must have sensed my desperation on the phone because she had picked a devotion to read to me and some Scripture to share. Honestly, I don't remember too much of what she read or what she said. But I do remember the love she showed me that day. There was no judging, no giving advice, no telling me to feel better. Just being sad with me and letting me talk and share how I was feeling. That's what I needed and God used her that afternoon. I will always remember her and love her for that. She became one of the biggest prayer warriors for me and Bill and one of the only people who I felt I could truly be open and honest with. She often prayed with me on the phone, something no one had ever done before. At first, it seemed awkward and uncomfortable, but I longed for those phone calls. She was taking time for me, and I could hear her prayer and burden for me. Once she even prayed and thanked God for my period! I quietly laughed, not understanding why she would be thankful for that. But as she prayed on, I realized she was thanking God that my body was still obviously producing eggs and going through the motions it should be going through. I also realized where she was coming from…finding some good in the situation and remembering to thank God for what I had, not blame Him for what I didn't have. It was a lesson that has stayed with me. I shared a great deal with her through this journey, and she will always have a special place in my heart. I love ya, Kimmy!

Even with the pain and grief, I wasn't ready to give up trying to be a mother. It was worth the risk of having to be disappointed again to try for another pregnancy. My doctors had not given us any reason to think I still couldn't have a healthy pregnancy, so I held on to that hope. We started trying again, but not as intensely. I tried to be more relaxed about it and not let it control my every thought. Our love life was beginning to suffer as a result of the goal of trying to conceive. Our love making had become not an expression of love, but a means to an end. It was mechanical. If we didn't feel like being romantic--tough! The calendar said we had to! That is not how it is supposed to be. When we were together, my thoughts were not on the moment, but on what time of the month it was, etc. If it wasn't the right time to conceive, I almost felt like "what's the point? Why bother." So, I tried to not let the calendar dictate when we made love. If we wanted to, we did. If we didn't want to, we didn't. I became pregnant again in December of that same year.

5
MY NIGHTMARE CONTINUES

I had suspected that I was pregnant, but I hadn't told Bill. Why make him worry until I knew for sure? I, myself, didn't really want to know. I didn't want to have to start the process of visiting the doctor and waiting again. But I needed to know. I bought a test and I think I kept it for a few days before using it. I finally told Bill that I thought I was pregnant and that I had bought a test and was going to take it. It was December 30, 2002. I went upstairs to perform the ritual, and it was positive. I went back downstairs and told Bill. We both said "okay," and that was that. We had become so guarded. There was no joy or excitement in the moment. That had been stolen from us forever. We would never have that innocent joy again.

I called my doctor the next day to make an appointment. He had said that I could take progesterone supplements the next time I became pregnant. He didn't say that was the reason for the miscarriages, but it wouldn't hurt. I made the appointment for January 2. On December 31, New Year's Eve, I started spotting. It had only been one day since the positive test! Why? Why was this happening again? Why couldn't everything be normal? I braced myself for the journey ahead; a journey I did not want to take again.

I saw the doctor on the second, and he did not seem concerned about the spotting. Again, he said spotting could be normal..blah, blah, blah. Hello???? Don't you remember what happened the past two times? Can't you do something? Do something to stop it from happening! Of course, my brain knew that there was absolutely nothing he could do to stop a miscarriage from happening. All he could do was treat it like it was normal until there was proof otherwise. My brain knew this; my heart did not. He gave me a prescription for the progesterone and I came home feeling beaten down and hopeless. I knew it was just a waiting game. My doctor had scheduled an ultrasound for six weeks. There should be a heartbeat by this time. There was not. He thought he saw something in my fallopian tube and suggested that it could be a tubal pregnancy. That's when the egg becomes fertilized, but does not make it through the tube into the uterus for some reason. He decided to do blood work again to test the hormone levels. The hormone levels double every 48 hours in a healthy pregnancy. In a tubal pregnancy, they increase, but only by a small amount. Mine did double, so the doctor was hopeful. But I still knew in the pit of my stomach that something was wrong.

I went for another ultrasound at seven weeks. There should definitely be a heartbeat now. I had gone by myself because I didn't want Bill to miss work. I had a feeling I was going to need him later. I had the same ultrasound technician as the times before and she was quiet, just as before. She took a long time and didn't say too much and then asked me to get dressed. I was waiting for the ball to drop. She called my doctor and he spoke to me on the phone. The technician had seen a heartbeat, but it was in my fallopian tube. It was a tubal pregnancy. He said I needed to have surgery right away before the tube burst and my life would be at risk. He told me to go straight to the hospital, and he would meet me there. I hung up the phone and just began sobbing uncontrollably. The nurses were wonderful to me. My doctor's nurse who knew me and knew my history, took me to his office and just hugged me. I needed that at that moment. I was by myself and trying to process the information of not only losing the pregnancy, but having to have major surgery again. She let me use the office phone to call Bill and my parents.

I had surgery that afternoon. I knew I had to have the surgery. It was not an option. My life was at risk and the baby could not grow inside of the tube. But it was still very difficult. With my other miscarriages, the babies had died on their own. This time, the surgery I agreed to have was going to end our baby's life. I felt a tremendous amount of guilt.

Physically, this surgery was easier to recover from than the first. Even though the doctor had to make an incision, I was up and moving around sooner and didn't need as much help doing things. The doctor was able to remove the pregnancy and save my tube, which was positive. I only had one tube now because the other one was removed with my first surgery. Hopefully, I could still get pregnant. There had been a fibrous cyst growing where the fallopian tube joins the uterus, and it was blocking the opening. The fertilized egg just couldn't get to where it needed to be. Again, I tried to focus on the positive. If I had never had the surgery, we could have tried for years to get pregnant and been unsuccessful, not knowing about the cyst.

My doctor still had two concerns, though. His first concern was that my tube was damaged from the surgery and would have scar tissue making it narrower and harder for an egg to pass through. He did a test in April after I had healed where he injected dye into the tube to see if it flowed through. Thankfully, it did. That meant my tube was open, and I could get pregnant again.

His second concern was that there would be a small amount of fetal tissue that had broken off somewhere in my body. That is a risk with removing a pregnancy from the tube. I had to go back in a few weeks for a post-operative check- up and to also have a pregnancy test to be sure it showed negative. The test still showed positive. He did some blood work to check hormone levels again. The levels were going down, but they were not as low as they should be. He was fairly certain there was fetal tissue growing somewhere. The next blood test showed my levels had increased. Now he knew for certain. He suggested a new procedure of giving an injection of methotrexate, a cancer drug used to kill off quickly growing cells. He had mentioned this to us as an option when he first suspected a tubal pregnancy, but by the time it was confirmed surgery was the only option. I had to have the injection now.

Technically, I was still pregnant, but the doctor didn't know where the tissue had lodged. If it kept growing, my life could be at risk and he would not know where to operate. I made the appointment at the cancer center to have the injection. Again, I felt so guilty. I knew it had to be done, but I still felt as if I were doing everything possible to destroy our baby. I knew there was not a baby anymore, just tissue, but my heart and my mind had become quite good at battling. Thinking straight and logically seemed to be a thing of the past. It took almost two months for the hormone level to go back to zero. That was a very difficult time having to go every week for a pregnancy test and seeing that it still showed positive. For so long, I had waited to see a positive test and now I wanted so badly for it to be negative so that the whole ordeal could be over.

I had lost three pregnancies now, but since the third one had been an ectopic pregnancy and not a miscarriage, I didn't qualify for the raised eyebrow of the medical world. They only seemed concerned after three consecutive miscarriages. My doctor had done a few tests after the second loss, some blood work and looking for basic and simple reasons. Everything had turned up normal. There was still no medical reason showing why I couldn't get pregnant again and have a healthy pregnancy. Of course, everyone I knew seemed to pull their medical license out of the closet and give me their opinion.

Emotionally, I was deeper into my nightmare and grief. I had fallen deeper into that pit and was seeing less and less sunlight. I was becoming grimier each day, and I reeked with the stench of misery and self-pity. I really tried to look at the positive side of things like the doctor finding my blocked tube and my tube still being healthy. But each time I tried to grab onto something positive and claw my way up the walls of the pit, dirt in the form of anger and bitterness would fall on my face and blind me. The walls would collapse a little more and I would slip back to the bottom. More and more I was losing my identity. I felt like I was wearing a huge sign around my neck for all the world to see, "I've had three miscarriages." All I seemed capable of talking about were my losses. "Can I take your order ma'am?" "Oh, I'll have a soda and a hamburger. And by the way, did you know that I've lost three pregnancies and had to have two surgeries?" Everything was about me and wanting people to feel sorry for me. I should have been putting that energy into dealing with my feelings and trying to heal. It would have been time better spent. But then God has a way of putting things in perspective, doesn't He?

6
BILL'S SURGERY

Only a few weeks after my surgery for the ectopic pregnancy, Bill started having severe lower/middle back pain. He had to sleep sitting up, and it was hard for him to stand or walk. He went to the doctor who assumed that he had pulled a muscle and prescribed muscle relaxers and physical therapy. The pain seemed to be too intense for just a pulled muscle, but he took the medicine and tried the therapy. It didn't help. The pain was worse. He could barely take baby steps at times. I remember one night, it took him almost thirty minutes to simply walk across the living room. Each step was such a chore and brought such severe pain. One night in bed, he couldn't even turn over. I had to tie a bed sheet onto the foot board of the bed for him to pull on to turn onto his side. Something was wrong. After a few weeks, the physical therapist noticed that the pain was the same, no improvement at all. She informed the doctor, and he ordered an MRI. The MRI was excruciating for him because he was not able to lie flat. The doctor had given him a prescription for a strong pain killer to take an hour before the test so that he could lie flat. It was as if he had taken a cough drop. I was just praying that the test would show what the problem was so that the doctor could fix it. It was very hard seeing him in so much pain and not being able to do one thing to help him. Bill had a feeling that something was wrong by the way the technician had acted. I was now the one feeling so helpless, the way I'm sure he had felt many times before. Our roles had been reversed.

Not long after we were home from the MRI, Bill's doctor called the house and told him that he had a tumor in his spinal column. A tumor? Did that mean cancer? He said it looked like an ependemoma, which is a benign tumor. He needed to have surgery soon and should not go back to work. He wanted to see him the next day, which was a Friday. Our heads were spinning. Tumor? Surgery? What did this mean? We had so many questions. Someone had pulled the carpet out from under us and then left us with our heads still trying to wrap around what we had been told. How were we supposed to wait until tomorrow to find out more information? The clock was going to tick so slowly. We remembered that a woman and dear friend from our church worked for a group of neurologists, so we called her. It was the same friend who had opened her home and heart to me on that gloomy and sad afternoon a few months back. Thankfully she was home and able to ease some of our concerns. It still seemed like forever until the next day.

We went to see Bill's doctor Friday morning. He said he didn't know too much about these tumors, but had read about them in several books. And then he said, "The survival rate is about five years," or something like that. I went pale and my stomach dropped. I sat down on the chair. What? I'm going to lose my husband? But we've had so little time together...there was so much more I want to do and share. My head was buzzing and a million thoughts and images were racing through my head. I was so scared. After talking with Bill, I learned that is not what he meant. But that is what he said. He meant that in these cases, after five years, there is an 80% chance of no re-occurrence. But I had had quite a wake-up call. The nurse made an appointment for us to see the neurologist on Monday. There we'd be able to get all of the information and have all of our questions answered. It was a very long weekend.

We had to wait for over two hours to see the doctor on Monday. He normally didn't see patients on Mondays; that was his surgery day. But he had made a special trip to the office for us. That told us how serious Bill's situation was. The doctor was very kind and very thorough in his explanation. He took his time with us and didn't seem to be in a hurry at all. He answered my legal pad full of questions and was very patient with us. Basically, Bill had a tumor growing in his spinal column that was large enough now to be pushing his spinal cord up against the wall of the spinal column. That is what was causing him so much pain. If he did not have surgery, the tumor would continue to grow and continue to push the spinal cord until he became paralyzed from that point down. He needed to have surgery immediately. The surgery also held several risks. The doctor could not tell from the MRI films if the tumor had grown into or around the spinal cord at all. He would not know until the surgery how easy it would be to remove. If he had to manipulate the spinal cord much, Bill could still be paralyzed. The risk was scary, but we knew he would become paralyzed for sure if he didn't have the surgery. The doctor confirmed that these types of tumors usually are slow growing and are usually benign. He said it was possible that the tumor could've been there since Bill was a baby. He scheduled the surgery for that Friday at 5:00 in the evening. He wanted to get the surgery in that week, so he had to add it on to the end of the week schedule. So we spent the week getting paperwork done for Bill's job and taking care of some things around the house to prepare for him to be laid up for a while. The doctor had said that the best case scenario would be for him to be off work for six weeks. Of course, it could be longer, depending on how the surgery went.

I don't think either of us spoke too much about our feelings that week. We were just about the business of taking care of things and getting things in order. I was very scared and worried, but I didn't want him to know that I was. I wanted to be strong for him. He was also scared and worried, but didn't want me to know. He wanted to be strong for me. I wish we would've just been open and honest with each other. It would've made the week a little easier to take if we faced our fears together instead of trying to hide them. We prayed together on Friday before leaving for the hospital and we both broke down in tears. The stress of the past week had caught up with us and we couldn't keep it buried any longer.

Bill had gone with me through two surgeries during the past two years, but I didn't realize how hard it was to be the spouse of someone having surgery. When you're the patient, surgery is a breeze. You're asleep through the whole thing. You don't have any idea what's happening to you or how much time has passed. You simply go to sleep and wake up when it's all over. On the other hand, if you're waiting for a loved one, especially a spouse, to have surgery, the clock is the enemy. Each minute that ticks by seems to last forever. And, of course, your mind wanders to think of all the 'what if's." One of the hardest parts for me was leaving him when they took him from his room to the surgery waiting area. I remember going to the family waiting area and finding my dad and just collapsing in his lap and bawling. It was so hard to let Bill go into someone else's care and to know that I couldn't be there with him. The surgery only lasted about an hour and a half, but it seemed like an eternity.

When the doctor finally came out to talk with me, he said everything went great. It couldn't have gone better. The tumor had popped right out totally intact. He did not have to manipulate the spinal cord at all. Praise God! He had told us at our visit that Bill may have to go to the neurological ICU after surgery for a few days, but he did so well, he went right to a regular room that night. What a weight that had been lifted! Some dear friends were there at the hospital waiting with us. We gathered in a circle in the middle of the waiting room and offered up prayers of thanksgiving.

Bill had to lie flat on his back for forty-eight hours after the surgery which was a huge chore. No pillows, no turning on his side, no nothing. He was very uncomfortable (and just a little grouchy!). I felt so bad for him. I knew how sore and uncomfortable he must have felt, but there was nothing I could do about it. It was just a fact that he had to deal with. His nurse Sunday night helped him to start sitting up slowly and by Monday morning, he was up walking. He surprised me when I got to the hospital that morning. When I had left Sunday night, he was absolutely miserable and making the nurses' jobs miserable too. What a change for only twelve hours! He was able to come home that afternoon. I was amazed. The doctor had talked about the neurological ICU, a possible several week hospital stay and possibly even a short stay at a rehabilitation hospital. Less than 72 hours after surgery he was home! Everything went as well and as smoothly as it could have. His recovery was about six weeks and was fairly easy. He still had a little pain, very minor compared to what it was before surgery, but that soon went away as the nerves relaxed. He was actually able to enjoy the time off from work. He could do most anything, except lift.

It has been over eight years since his surgery as I write these words, and he has had no complications at all. His back does get tired easily if he stands for long periods of time because they had to remove a few bones in his back so his spine has been compromised a bit. But that is a very manageable consequence considering he could've been in a wheel chair the rest of his life. He is under the care and surveillance of a neuro-oncologist for the next ten years. He has had to go every two years for an MRI to scan and be sure the tumor is not re-growing or re-appearing anywhere.

I tell you this story because looking back God used this situation to put things in perspective for me. It took the focus off of me and put it on someone else. I couldn't think of myself during these few months. I had to focus on Bill and his surgery and recovery and his doctor appointments and medications and all that went along with it. I didn't have time to feel sorry for myself and to focus on what I didn't have. God was making me look at what I did have. I do feel badly for Bill that he had to be the object for my lesson. After those months, I did begin to look at things a little differently. I certainly wasn't out of the pit by any means. I was still grieving and still had issues I hadn't dealt with. It was still very difficult for me to see babies or to be around babies or pregnant women. But I had learned to stop and thank God for the gifts in my life once in a while, though. That was something I had forgotten how to do.

"Be joyful always; pray continually; give thanks in all circumstances, for this is God's will for you in Christ Jesus." 1 Thessalonians 5:16-18

"" For everything God created is good." 1 Timothy 4:4

7
MORE HEARTACHE

Late that summer, one of my best friends called to tell me she was pregnant. SLAM! It hit me hard and knocked me on my rear. I could hardly respond to her. I muttered, "I'm happy for you," not knowing what else to say, hung up the phone, and cried hard and long. She had only been married for a little over a year. I didn't even know they were trying to have a family. We had been trying longer than they had even been dating. This wasn't fair! Why was it so easy for them and so hard for us? My anger grew and simmered and finally boiled over late one night. I found myself at the computer writing an e-mail to her. Unfortunately, she became the object of some major anger and resentment issues that I had kept buried. It wasn't her that I was angry with; it was the situation. I don't remember the words that I fired off that night, but I remember the gist of the e-mail. It was not nice. In fact, it was rather nasty and mean. In a nutshell, I told her that I wasn't happy for them and how I thought everyone should have to suffer just as we had. I said I didn't want to hear about the pregnancy or hear about baby stuff. I regret sending that e-mail now and would give anything to take it back. It was my anger and unresolved grief talking, not me. Thankfully, our friendship is strong, and she (with a little help from her dear husband, I think) realized that I was just lashing out and has forgiven me. I am lucky and blessed to have such an understanding friend who is there through all of the rough times. Annabelle, you're one in a million!

Spiritually, it was a continual battle between head and heart. In my head, I knew God was not a vengeful God or a God who exasperated his children. I knew that He had a plan for us and that He loved us. I knew that I needed to continue thanking Him for the blessings He had given us and continue asking for the child that I ached to hold and to love. I knew that He heard my prayers. My heart wasn't always on the same page. I had so much grief, pain, anger, resentment, and fear bottled up inside that it clouded my spiritual knowledge. I was feeling very frustrated with praying and asking for God to grant our heart's desire. I was beginning to feel it was pointless and a waste of time to pray. God certainly knew what we wanted. Why should I keep asking Him and telling Him over and over again when obviously He had his own plan in mind? He hadn't answered my prayers up to this point. He had allowed me to lose three babies. I struggled every day with this issue. I never strayed from my faith in God or turned away from Him or stopped loving Him. I did, however, have questions for Him, and I was angry with Him. As I said earlier in the book, I loved Him, I just didn't like what He was doing and how He was going about it. How I longed for a burning bush! I prayed so fervently that God would show me what his plan was;

that somehow He would reveal to me why I had to suffer these losses and heartbreaks. Of course, God does not work like that. That's where our faith and trust comes into play. I knew I had to just keep plugging along blindly trusting that God knew what was best for us and that he had something wonderful and amazing in store for us if we just kept leaning on Him.

"I lift up my eyes to the hills-where does my help come from? My help comes from the Lord, the Maker of heaven and earth." Psalm 121:1-2

Church services proved to be difficult again for several reasons. One was simply the crowd factor. I wasn't comfortable being around people, especially a large group, for whatever reason. I never felt more alone than when I was in a room full of people. I know that sounds strange, and it's difficult to put into words the way I felt in those situations. I wanted people to acknowledge my pain, but I didn't. I wanted people to ask me how I was doing, but I didn't. I wanted people to hug me and cry with me, but I didn't. I wanted people to leave me alone and just let me be, but I didn't. My emotions were so torn. So I tended to stay away from social situations, no matter the reason.

Another reason the services were difficult was because I couldn't get through a song service without losing it and crying. My emotions were so raw and close to the surface, including my spiritual emotions. Singing about God and His love just brought all of those emotions to the top and they spilled out. Why is it that people are uncomfortable crying in church? (Or at least that had been my experience up to this point.) Isn't that supposed to be a safe and loving place? I heard someone say one time that a trembling upper lip is more of a sign of a Christian than a stiff upper lip. I believe that is so true. Yet, I felt as if it was a sign of weakness if I cried. I felt as if I would be letting people know that I wasn't as strong as I was pretending to be. Was everyone else pretending too? Wasn't there anyone besides me who was hurting and struggling? So I would sit and try to fight back the tears that were determined to flow. I would walk up to the church doors as the hurting and grieving me and when I walked through the doors I was the award winning actress. I would paint on my happy smile, throw my shoulders back, push down all of the nasty emotions and begin reciting my lines that I had rehearsed. I was pretty good at pretending and acting the part of a woman who had it all together and remarkably strong. I was able to make everyone believe that I had dealt with the losses and maybe deep down I hoped that my pretending would slowly become my reality. Of course the show was exhausting. I couldn't wait for the curtain to drop so that I could be myself again, take off the make-up and let my hair down, put on my old clothes of self-pity and bitterness. That's when I was comfortable.

We should be able to confess our sins and our struggles to one another as Christians. But, it seems when we do, generally speaking, they judge us, as if they were perfect. In fact, when we confess our sins to one another, everyone should be waving their hands in the air and shouting, "Me too!! Me too!!"

"Therefore confess your sins to each other and pray for each other so that you may be healed. The prayer of a righteous man is powerful and effective." James 5:16

"You, therefore, have no excuse, you who pass judgment on someone else, for at whatever point you judge the other, you are condemning yourself, because you who pass judgment do the same things." Romans 2:1

"As it is written, 'there is no one righteous, not even one'. Romans 3:10

Another reason I shied away from church was the family aspect. Everywhere I looked there were families and family activities and kids hugging their moms and dads. It was just too much to see. I avoided babies, kids, and families at all costs during the week…on television, at the supermarket, even with my friends. So why would I make an exception on Sundays? It was like a slap in the face when I would see families sitting together and see the joy on the face of new parents. One Sunday, I remember sitting in the pew, and I was doing fairly well and holding it together. I had learned to keep my mind somewhat focused on other things and just go through the motions. (Another reason why I felt going to services was pointless. I wasn't listening and I was getting nothing out of it. I was thinking about what I needed from the grocery store or remembering a vacation that Bill and I had taken just to get through.) After the service had started, a family with a newborn baby came in and sat down right in front of me. Well, that's all it took for me to lose it and begin crying. The flood gates had opened. I had to get up and leave the sanctuary, and I spent the rest of the service in the restroom. My parents had come with us that Sunday morning for some reason, and I hated that I fell apart in front of them. Of course, it was a good thing. I think they realized how much I was hurting and how difficult even simple things were for me. From that Sunday on, I always sat in the very last pew so that I could exit quickly and without being noticed. Most times, we arrived just in time for the service to start, and we left during the final hymn. I wanted to avoid as much as possible.

It was very frustrating that people saw this emotional issue as a spiritual issue. I can't tell you how many times I was preached to by well meaning church friends about my "straying." I would try to explain that I wasn't avoiding God, I was avoiding the social situation. But no one seemed to understand. How could they? I felt as if I was expected not to grieve because I was a Christian. The people in the church made me feel like because of my faith, I was supposed to just accept the loses as God's plan, maybe cry for a moment or two, but then put a smile on my face and get on with being happy because I was a child of God. I never felt like I had permission from the Christian world to grieve and be sad and feel angry and question why this was happening. I never felt permission to grieve over the possibility of not ever being a mother and giving my husband, whom I love more than anything, a child. This was the root, I believe, of my pretending. And as crazy as it sounds, I needed permission, verbal or otherwise, to show my true feelings. I needed someone to say to me, "It's okay to be sad. It's okay to feel miserable and hopeless." I needed to face all of those feelings that I had been trying to hold back and pretending they didn't exist. I needed to come face to face with them, stare at them head on, realize their ugliness, before I could ever begin to heal.

I was also very disappointed in the church we were attending at that time. If it appeared from the outside that I was straying and on the "outs" with God, why weren't people talking to me and praying with me and offering guidance and encouragement? I would become so angry on Sunday mornings listening to the leaders in the pulpit talk about our visitors and how important they were. I would want to scream when I heard people talking about ways to reach our neighbors and the hurting people of the community. Yes, I believe all that is true and it is our calling as Christians to witness to those who need Christ in their lives. But I couldn't help feeling abandoned by my own church. There was such a focus on bringing people in that they were overlooking tending to the ones who were already there. I felt so strongly about it that I decided to write a letter to our minister and to our church leaders explaining how I felt. It wasn't a letter of complaint, but a letter of concern and suggestions for how they could possibly improve on tending to the flock. I was very disheartened to not get a response. They didn't seem to care that a member of their congregation was hurting and trying to reach out for help. There was one elder who admitted that he felt uncomfortable talking about "women's issues." I gently reminded him that this wasn't a "women's issue." It was a hurting and grieving issue. I promised there would be no formal discussion of my uterus involved. In my opinion, an elder should be mature enough to realize that. It was during this time that Bill and I decided we needed to find a more nurturing and prayerful congregation. We have since moved on from that church, and the Lord has led us to a church that has several families that have had fertility problems. It's not something that is kept quiet and not talked about and swept under the carpet. It's a real issue that real people, including faithful Christians, struggle with. We thank God continually for leading us to this healing and loving church.

In September of that year, 2003, Bill and I were baptized again. We had both become Christians as children and were baptized with no true understanding of what it meant to be a Christian. Our faith in God had never been tried and tested the way it had over the past few years. Even though we didn't understand God and His ways didn't make sense to us, we felt closer to Him and felt our faith had been strengthened. We wanted to recommit ourselves to Him and to experience baptism with a renewed trust and giving of ourselves. It was not an act of feeling that we needed to be saved again; it was an act of recommitment. I liken it to people renewing their wedding vows. When you and your spouse recite those vows to one another, you have no idea what they mean. You have a naïve idea of what "for better or for worse" means. After twenty-five years of marriage, those same words have a whole new meaning because you've lived through the better and the worse. Saying your vows to one another after years of marriage simply emphasizes to your mate that you know the meaning of staying together through it all and that your love for them transcends all that life can throw at you. Our baptism was a symbol that we were committed to Christ even when life was uncertain and everything seemed to not make sense. It was an intimate and private service with only a few people. We didn't share our decision with many people, but I felt it was important to include this in the story of my journey.

I found my time with God at home. After my third pregnancy loss and surgery, I stayed in our bedroom most of the time. I found it comforting to listen to my Christian music CDs. It was a constant reminder to me of God's love and of His presence. I also kept the radio downstairs on the Christian music station. Again, it was comforting and peaceful in a way to always have songs of praise and songs that quoted Scripture playing in the background. It gave me something to focus on and helped get me through many a day. We had a screened porch on the back of the house that I claimed as my refuge. I spent many hours sitting in the rocking chair on the porch listening to the birds singing and talking to God. It was a peaceful and quiet place where I could contemplate and commune with the Lord. It was just me and Him. I didn't have to pretend, and I could be raw and honest. I would also use this time on the porch to read my Bible and write in my journal. It's hard to admit, but I would sometimes be sad when Bill would come home from work because I knew my time on the porch had to come to an end for the day. I needed to take care of him and see to some kind of dinner.

But I knew I would have the next day to once again enjoy the solitude and the comforting arms of my porch.

"The Lord is close to the brokenhearted and saves those who are crushed in spirit." Psalm 34:18

8
FERTILITY SPECIALIST

We visited a fertility doctor in April of 2003 after I had the dye test performed on my remaining fallopian tube to see if it was opened. My doctors were wonderful, and I was happy with everything they had done. We just wanted the opinion of a doctor who specialized in fertility problems. I don't recall him doing any kind of physical exam. I believe he reviewed the information our doctors had sent to him, including all of the tests we had had done. We talked with him for a while, and he was a little encouraging. He told us that the two miscarriages (the ectopic pregnancy didn't count) were totally common and normal. Women in their thirties experience a miscarriage one in every three pregnancies. My chances of having another one were almost the same as if I had never had one. He said my tube looked healthy, and that there was only a fifteen percent chance of having another tubal pregnancy due to some scar tissue. He spent quite a bit of time discussing in vitro fertilization. That is a process where the eggs, usually four to five, are fertilized outside of the body and then placed in the womb. They use medication to try to produce healthier eggs and to produce more than normal during a cycle. This increases the chances of getting pregnant and hopefully weeds out unhealthy eggs. He estimated our chances of getting pregnant on our own at about forty percent. He suggested that if we wanted to continue trying on our own, to go ahead, but to come back to see him in six months if we had not succeeded.

The idea of in vitro did not appeal to us that April. It was very expensive and was not covered by our insurance. The success rate given to us was only 50/50. That was only about a 10% greater chance than trying on our own. I hadn't had trouble getting pregnant. It was keeping the pregnancy. There was also an increased chance of twins since more than one egg would be implanted. Actually, neither of us was too put off by the idea of twins. We had worked so hard and been through so much already just trying to conceive one baby; having two with one pregnancy seemed like a good idea. We could have the two children we wanted and move on with our lives. But, it didn't seem the answer for us at that time. We filed the information away and tried to back away from the whole situation for a while. I believe it was also during this spring that we had some more tests done. My regular ob/gyn wanted to be sure that our chromosomes were a match and not ones that would for some reason always create unhealthy embryos. That test came back completely normal. I stayed on birth control for the next several months. I needed a break from the whole situation.

We had two dogs at this point in our lives, both basset hounds. One we had brought into our home as a puppy, Abby; the other we had adopted through the rescue with which we volunteered, Sassy. She was an old sweet girl who had been abused, neglected, and not very loved. It took her a while to gain trust in us and allow us to get close to her and love on her. She had become my shadow. She went everywhere in the house I went. She was always by my side and at times would look up to me as if to say "thank you for loving me and taking care of me." She could melt my heart. We only had her for a little less than three years before we lost her to cancer. It was a tremendous blow to me. I loved her. It was another loss. It was another failure, another being I could not protect and save. I cried for days for her, for me. I cried myself to sleep for many nights. I missed her constant presence and comfort she gave. It was more grief.

CHAPTER NINE-LINDA

B ill's mom, Linda, lived about forty-five minutes away from us in an apartment condo. We were close to her, even though we didn't see each other too often or spend a great deal of time together. We talked on the phone quite a bit and stayed up to date with what was going on. She had some health issues which kept us from going places and doing things together, but we knew she was always there emotionally and spiritually for us. She was a strong Christian woman and had done an amazing job of raising Bill and his sister on her own since they were very small. She had always been active in church going to Bible studies and teaching Sunday School and directing Vacation Bible School. Her faith was strong and she loved the Lord dearly. She also was an excellent mother-in-law! We lived with her for the first year we were married. Her house had a separate side entrance that led to the upstairs and could be closed off from the downstairs by a door. Neither of us had good paying jobs when we were married. We had only been out of college for three months. Bill was working part-time at a local radio station doing weekend overnight shifts, and I was trying to get established in the school district where we lived by getting my name on the substitute teaching list.

I was lucky to get called one day a week for the first few months. Needless to say, we didn't have much money. Linda knew how much we wanted to get married and how we had stuck by our commitment to finish college first. So she offered to let us turn the upstairs of her house into an apartment and let us live there for free for as long as we needed. What a blessing! We spent a few hundred dollars and lots of elbow grease on some paint and new carpet. One of the rooms had been used as storage, so we made countless trips down to the basement (and out to the curb!) carrying all kinds of boxes and old furniture. That room already had a sink and counter in it, I guess where someone had used it as a separate apartment some time earlier. We had a friend install an outlet for a stove and bought a used refrigerator and stove for $100.00. Bill's old bedroom became our living room and his sister's old bedroom became our bedroom. The bathroom had an old claw foot tub, so we had to do some tweaking to be able to use it as a shower. We didn't have air conditioning, but we had a window unit in the living room and bedroom. Neither of them worked very well, but if we sat right in front of them, we managed to stay relatively cool. We had our own phone line and cable, so we were able to live independently of Bill's mom except for having to go to the basement to do our laundry. It wasn't a fancy place by any means. It was simple and humble, and we had to be creative to find places for everything, but it was home and we liked it. I don't think we would have been able to get married when we did if it had not been for Linda's generosity. She helped us get a good start in our life together. We were able to save some money, and, more importantly, we didn't have to spend the little that we had saved trying to scrape by day to day. That was a wonderful gift. So we lived above her for a little over a year. We would go sometimes for a few weeks without even seeing each other. We were enjoying being newlyweds and having our own place together and living in our "newlywed bubble." Her bedroom window was in the very front of the tall, skinny house which sat very close to the street. We usually parked on the street in front of her window, and sometimes, if her window was open, we would exchange hellos and chit chat for a few minutes. She was so respectful of our space and of our time together. She didn't have any expectations for us, like coming downstairs to join her for dinner all the time or coming upstairs to our apartment all of the time. I can't even really remember more than a time or two that she visited us upstairs. She never meddled or interfered with our lives. We were occupying the same house, but she allowed us to have our privacy and our space. She was there if we needed her, but she took a very hands-off backseat approach. I never asked her later on if that was difficult for her to do. I don't suspect it was. That was the kind of person she was. She loved Bill and she loved me and she wanted us to be able to start building our life together on our own. When Bill landed a good paying stable job, and I was hired for my first full-time teaching job, we moved out and rented an apartment. I think she put her house on the market the next day! We did not know that she wanted to move into a condo. She kept that to herself and stayed in the house until we moved out.

Linda had had surgery in January of 2003. She had decided after years and years of weight loss programs to have gastric bypass surgery. It was her last resort. She had battled with weight issues all of her adult life and had even tried a radical doctor- controlled diet where she was only allowed to drink nutritional shakes for a period of a few months. It was a tough program, but she stuck to it and was successful at losing quite a bit of weight. This was maybe a year before Bill and I were married. She found freedom that she hadn't known for a very, very long time. She started having a social life, outside of church, and doing things with her friends. She went on several trips, one of which was a Christian cruise for singles. It took a lot of courage for her to book a trip on a cruise by herself. She was going it alone. Her weight loss had given her back her confidence and it showed. She was beaming with pride in herself and with a new energy. Unfortunately, when people overeat, there are always underlying emotional issues. I think Linda tried to deal with those issues. She never talked too much about them to her family, but I know she saw a counselor over the years. I don't know how intensely she tried to deal with them and overcome them, or even to recognize them. I do know that the issues stayed when the weight left, and eventually the weight came back. She was miserable, trapped inside a body that she hated and becoming more and more depressed and frustrated each year. I believe she finally decided to do something physically to try to over ride the problems. That's when the gastric bypass surgery seemed to be the answer for her.

She was sixty-one when the surgery was performed, a bit older than the average patient. Her doctor told her of his concerns, but she insisted he go ahead with it and he did. The actual procedure went fine, but she never fully recovered. She was never able to eat solid foods again. She was constantly nauseated and vomiting. Her doctor did not seem concerned and said it would get better with time. Over the next year, she became weaker and less able to take care of herself. She was admitted to the hospital a few times and several different nursing homes and had made the decision to sell her condo and move to an assisted living facility. We packed up her condo, except for the basics that she could take with her to the assisted living facility. I don't remember all the details or the order of all the events, but somewhere along the way, she decided that she wasn't ready to give up her independence and move to a "home." She wanted to give it all she had and try one more time to make it work living on her own. Bill and I and Bill's sister supported her in any decision she made. We talked through all of the benefits and drawbacks, but ultimately, it was her choice. We couldn't take away her life. So, we moved her back home. I spent a lot of time with her trying to figure out what she could eat without getting sick and helping her physically to try to get her strength back. I spent time with her at the hospital when she was there talking to nurses and social workers and therapists and trying to help her keep up with her personal bills, etc. I don't tell you this to ask for a pat on the back. I did what I needed to do for my mother-in-law and would do it all again. I wanted her to be happy and to be able to go back to work and to be involved in church again. I tell you this because it was another way God spoke to me and showed me that life isn't all about me. We had decided to take a break from trying to get pregnant in January of '03, and then God gave me somebody else and another situation to care about and to take care of. I needed to take care of Bill's mom. And so I spent eight or nine months focusing on someone else and putting my worries and problems aside. It was good for me, physically and emotionally. She gave me a reason to get out of bed each morning, a purpose for my day. So physically, I was dressed and out of the house and back among the living again. Emotionally, I had too much to think about with her to dwell on my own unhappiness for too long.

Linda went home to be with the Lord on January 19 of 2004. She died peacefully in her sleep in her own home, which is where she wanted to be. It was a great shock to us, but a comfort in a sense because we knew that she was no longer battling demons that she had fought for so long. She was with Jesus, which is where I believe she so deeply longed to be. She taught me a great lesson of faith. With all of her struggles with her weight and issues and tough times of being a single mom and raising two kids on her own, she never, ever gave up on God or questioned His love and provisions. She stayed faithful through it all and fought the good fight. I chose 2 Timothy 4:7-8 to be printed on her funeral memorial cards, and I still think of her whenever I hear or read the verse. *"I have fought the good fight, I have finished the race, I have kept the faith. Now there is in store for me the crown of righteousness, which the Lord, the righteous judge, will award to me on that day–and not only to me, but also to all who have longed for his appearing."*

10
GLIMPSE OF HOPE

After our vacation in July of 2003, I decided I was ready to start trying again. By September, I was already frustrated. Taking a break had been good, but it didn't take long to sink right back into the anger and frustration of the month to month waiting game. It was like I had come up from out of the water and took a nice breath after gasping and struggling and thinking I was going to die and then I was pulled right back under by the same weight for it all to start again. I knew what was coming. I knew the pain of struggling and gasping for breath and feeling out of control and knowing this was the end, and I didn't want to go back there.

I was beginning to lean more toward in-vitro. It was so stressful trying to figure out my fertile time each month and then to schedule sex during that small window, in the mood or not. And then having the disappointment of feeling the cramps and seeing the blood on the toilet paper and knowing all of the planning did not work and we would have to start over. At least with in-vitro, all of the timing and planning is done for you. They give you medications to manipulate your ovaries and your body the way they want. The doctors control the timing. It wouldn't be my fault if it didn't work; it would be theirs. The risk for another tubal pregnancy would also be gone since the procedure bypasses the tubes all together. It was looking more and more like the best choice for us. I wanted to be sure that we had done all that we could do, though, before moving in that direction. I went to see my doctor in November to discuss with him that we were flirting with the idea of in-vitro. He said it would be completely normal for a couple in our situation to take up to a year and a half to get pregnant. A year and a half! That was like telling me twenty years. It was a lifetime. It was forever. I was losing my patience with the whole fertility game and needed something to happen soon or I was going to lose it. He gave me a prescription for Chlomid, a fertility drug, for four months. He said that he didn't expect it to increase my chances a great deal, but that it wouldn't hurt. The drug simply makes sure that you are ovulating, and he was fairly certain that I was. It was his thought that Bill's sperm just couldn't get to the egg because of my damaged tube. That doesn't make much sense to me now as I am writing about it because the test that I had done on my tube earlier that year showed that it was open. If the sperm couldn't get to the egg, how did he expect the egg to make the long journey back down the tube to the womb? Of course, I think with a bit more clarity now than I did then. Anyway, he also suggested that Bill have his sperm tested. He didn't think that was an issue, but it would be one more test and one more possible reason to cross off of our list. The test came back normal.

The Chlomid did absolutely nothing except give me hot flashes and make me feel like more of a part of the infertility world. Everyone, and I mean everyone, had taken Chlomid. I felt like an official member now. I had taken fertility drugs. My infertility was now validated.

That December, we began going to Resolve meetings, an infertility support group. Bill went with me. I wanted him to. I needed him to. I couldn't do this by myself. I wanted us to face this together and to meet other couples who also struggled with the pain of wanting a family, but having bodies that would not cooperate for one reason or another. He, of course, was totally there for me and for whatever I needed of him.

Our first meeting was in the home of the couple who had been leading the chapter in our city. It's such a bizarre feeling….we were going to a complete stranger's house, yet we felt a connection to them already. We knew walking up to the door that they had experienced heartbreak and tears and anger and pain and isolation because they were members of this group that no one ever wants to become members of. We knew that they were going to understand and relate to us like no one had ever done before. And we were right. They welcomed us into their home with open arms and hearts. We spent a few minutes just talking lightly about general stuff, knowing in the back of our minds the heavy and hard stuff was coming. There were a few more people there; I really don't remember. I think there were a few women there by themselves because their husbands couldn't or didn't want to come. We finally all sat down in their living room and went around the group one at a time telling our stories. It was similar to the experience of the grief support group I had gone to a few times. It was so freeing to be able to talk and share and cry and know that the people listening truly understood the pain and heartache. They understood how difficult and painful it was to be around the kids in the family and to see and hear about friends getting pregnant at the drop of a hat and to have to avoid baby showers and baby stores and baby commercials and baby anything. They knew how difficult it was for me to see other pregnant women. They had felt the sting of knowing a young teenage girl was permitted to have a baby, but yet we were denied. They felt the same anger at their bodies that I felt for it not working the way it was supposed to. They felt the guilt for not being able to give their husband a child. We could have talked all night, but, of course, the evening had to end. We left there with a feeling of relief and gratitude knowing that there were other people we could finally share with. I was already counting the days until our next monthly meeting.

We had endured three pregnancy losses now and, although they were extremely painful and difficult, we did not feel ready to give up, or I should say I did not feel ready to give up. Bill had made it clear several times that whatever I decided was fine with him. He knew how tough the past few years had been on me, emotionally and physically, and was willing to accept whatever decision I made. I still felt it was worth the risk to try again, even if it failed. I wanted so desperately to be a mother. It was all I thought about. The past three and a half years had been consumed by it. I couldn't give up and walk away. I had invested too much. I did feel, however, that I needed to take a more active roll in trying to be a parent. I couldn't just sit back anymore and leave it all up to chance. I needed to DO something; do something to help it happen; do as much as I possibly could to be sure I became pregnant again and that it would be a healthy pregnancy. I needed to feel some degree of control; like I was in charge of my body in some way.

So, in January of 2004, we decided to give in-vitro fertilization a try. We had visited a fertility doctor in the spring of 2003, and he had discussed in-vitro with us, but we had not been ready to travel down that road then. We had been able to conceive on our own. The doctors and all the tests showed no reason why we would not be able to again. Plus the in-vitro process was quite a lot to digest and comprehend….all the shots and medications and timing and procedures. And there was the issue of what to do with any fertilized eggs that were not implanted. They were the beginnings of life. We could not destroy them. That would go against our moral and spiritual beliefs. But that was 2003. This was 2004. I was desperate. I had to cling to some hope, and this was it. It was my last chance. It just had to work.

We also prayed about it. I remember coming home from the informational meeting in January, and Bill and I both praying together asking for God to help us make this decision, to show us if this was the path He wanted us to take. We asked that He show us clearly if in-vitro wasn't part of His plan for us. It felt right. All of our questions from the doctor had been answered. We no longer felt the hesitation and uncertainty we had felt before.

"Commit your way to the Lord; trust in Him." Psalm 37:5

And so we went to the beginner's class at the infertility clinic and learned all about the process and about the medications and the shots. Bill actually practiced giving an orange a shot, just like we had heard about. We watched a video about how the eggs are harvested and joined with the sperm in a Petri dish and then implanted back into the womb. We learned about a program where you can donate your frozen unused eggs to other couples who need healthy eggs. That meant we didn't need to destroy them. With in-vitro, you are given medications to help produce healthier eggs. That means the chances of having a miscarriage are less. The egg would also not have to travel in my tube, so the chances of another tubal pregnancy were zero. All of this sounded very appealing to us, and so we decided to begin the journey. There was still the financial risk, but we both felt it was worth it if it would give us the baby we had been longing for. All we had to do now was wait for my period to start so that I could begin taking the medications.

11
AN ANSWERED PRAYER
AND MORE PAIN

My period didn't start. My cycles were not consistent every month, so I never knew exactly when I would start. I waited and then waited a few more days. Then I took the home pregnancy test. It was positive. How amazing! Now I didn't have to go through all of the poking and prodding and shots. This was wonderful! God had spared us the financial risk. God had told us that in vitro was not the way intended for us to have a family.

"Wait for the Lord; be strong and take heart and wait for the Lord." Psalm 27:14

I called my regular ob/gyn, and we began the routine of doing blood work. Every other day I had to go to the office for the nurse to draw blood and then wait by the phone for the doctor to call to give me the hormone levels. The news, of course, was not good. My levels were not doubling as they should be. My doctor was suspicious of another tubal pregnancy due to the blood test results. He suggested trying the methotrexate drug to terminate the pregnancy. I asked if he could do surgery and just remove my remaining tube so that I wouldn't have to deal with this again. I certainly didn't want to go through surgery again, but I felt like this was the only option for me. I needed to let my body know that I was finished with this awful game of trying to conceive and having a healthy pregnancy. I just wanted my insides to be ripped out and end this nightmare. If my tube was gone, I couldn't get pregnant. I didn't have to make the decision mentally whether to try again or to close the door on the whole situation. I didn't think I was capable of making the decision myself to just stop trying. This would make the decision for me. End of story.

My doctor told me that he should be able to perform the surgery laproscopically, which requires only three small cuts, so the recovery time is relatively short. That was good news. At least I didn't have to go through the pain of another incision. So we scheduled the procedure for later that week.

I woke from the surgery and heard the sound of Bill's voice. What? What was he saying? It sounded like he was saying that the doctor didn't remove my tube. That couldn't be. I wanted it gone. I tried to focus a little more from my groggy state. Yes. That is what he said. The pregnancy had not been a tubal one after all, so my tube was healthy, and he did not remove it. I felt like I had been punched in the stomach, not from the physical pain, but knowing that my nightmare was going to continue. The story wasn't over. I remember my dad leaning over me and rubbing my head and saying it was going to be okay. I looked up at him and asked if he ever just prayed for Jesus to return. That is what I wanted. I didn't want to continue down this path of pain and hopelessness. I was tired. Tired of the pain. Tired of the disappointments. Tired of the effort. Tired of the fear. Tired of the heartache. Tired of the emptiness, anger, resentment, guilt, helplessness. I just wanted it all to end. I longed for Heaven. I craved the Scriptures that spoke of Christ's return and the joy of being with Him forever. I couldn't seem to read enough of the verses that talked about every tear being wiped away and that there would be no more sadness. ***"Weeping may remain for a night, but rejoicing comes in the morning."*** ***Psalm 30:5*** The thought of having to live with the pain was almost unbearable. I never considered taking my own life, though I believe I caught a glimpse into the world of a person who has contemplated that escape. I did, however, pray for Jesus to come and end my pain. I prayed that prayer a lot.

"For the Lord himself will come down from heaven, with a loud command, with the voice of the archangel and with the trumpet call of God, and the dead in Christ will rise first. After that, we who are still alive and are left will be caught up together with them in the clouds to meet the Lord in the air. And so we will be with the Lord forever. 1 Thessalonians 4:16-17

The next month or two were very, very dark. I cried a great deal. It was a challenge to go through the day to day routine of taking care of Bill and the house. I didn't go out very much. My happiest place was just lying in bed with Bill, holding him and him holding me. I wanted to stay there forever and cocoon with him. I was just existing. I was missing out on life. I wasn't able to enjoy my family, my friends or any situation. I was simply going through the motions of surviving minute by minute. When you are in survival mode, there is nothing else that matters except getting through the next hour and sometimes the next minute. It takes all of your energy to put one foot in front of the other and to function as a seemingly sane person. I had no desire to see anyone or talk to anyone. I slept a great deal. That was the easiest way to deal with the day…be unconscious. I didn't feel when I was sleeping. I felt no one could begin to understand how I was feeling and the intensity of my pain and sadness. Everything, and I mean everything, somehow reminded me of my barren and uncooperative body. From doing laundry that did not contain any baby clothes to driving a car that did not contain a car seat to cleaning a house that did not contain any baby furniture or toys, everything and every situation seemed to shout loudly and clearly, "You're a failure!" The loneliness and emptiness had engulfed my whole being. I remember sitting in the waiting room of my ob/gyn office that April and looking around and noticing that all of the other women who were waiting were pregnant (or so it seemed). The walls began to close in, and I could feel myself fighting to keep my composure. I wanted to look at their pregnant bellies, but looking at them made my stomach sick and my heart ache. A young pregnant teenage girl sitting next to me was wobbling after her toddler and commenting to her mother how she wasn't looking forward to "having another kid" to chase after. She herself was a child. She complained about her swollen ankles and her aching back and her lack of sleep. All of the other expectant mothers seemed to nod in agreement and aggravation. My heart was pounding and my face was hot. I wanted to stand up right in the middle of the room and scream at all of them, "Don't you know how lucky you are? Don't you realize what a gift you've been given? How can you sit there and complain? Don't you know the pain I've been through and what I wouldn't give to have those problems?" Well, of course, they didn't. I could feel the tears welling up, and I tried with all I had to hold them back. The nurse came to the door and called my name. I stood up, walked into the hall, and burst into tears. I tried to explain through my sobbing what had upset me and why I was crying. The nurse just stood there looking at me, trying to figure out why this patient had lost it at the simple calling of her name. I guess she was finally able to put the pieces of broken words together, sort through my sobs, and get a grasp on my meltdown. She put her arm around me and hugged me for a while, letting me cry. She had been there through the past few years, and she knew my situation. She was very kind and comforting, but I felt like an absolute idiot. I was in a pit that I knew I could not climb out of by myself.

"Save me, O God, for the waters have come up to my neck. I sink in the miry depths, where there is no foothold. I have come into the deep waters; the floods engulf me. I am worn out calling for help; my throat is parched. My eyes fail, looking for God." Psalm 69:1–3

12
THE LETTER

I believe it was sometime during the early spring months of 2004 that I sent a letter to my family and close friends. At the infertility support group meetings, we talked a lot about how our family and friends did not understand how we were feeling, what we were dealing with, and the thousands of little ways infertility affected our daily lives. We could not expect them to, but at times, we longed for them to be able to wipe away the dirt and grime and filth and be able to peer into the window of our soul. But as much as we longed for them to know our pain, it was impossible to share with them. When a situation arose that was difficult or painful for us to face and our wounds once again laid open, it was too difficult to explain to others in that moment. And part of us would feel angry that we had to explain, that those close to us couldn't see how that particular situation would be painful.

One of the women from the support group had come up with a letter that she sent to all of her family and friends explaining some of the difficult times during the year and difficult situations. She wanted to let everyone know upfront, before the situation arose, to clue them into things that were obvious in our world of infertility, but not so obvious to everyone else. It was a great idea, and I couldn't wait to mail my copy. Finally, an easy and quick way to help those closest to me get a glimpse and an understanding of what I needed.

One of the points the letter made was that attending baby showers and observing Mother's Day were no longer an option. Going to a baby shower meant pretending to be happy and excited, while at the same time, the dagger in my heart was being turned and twisted. It was an unnecessary event that would lead to knocking me off my already unstable feet and take days to recover. It just wasn't worth it. Mother's Day was simply rubbing salt in the wound, and I would not be going anywhere that day, especially to church. Seeing all the moms wearing corsages from their children and having to sit and watch mothers embrace their little ones as they were handed an "I love mom" craft from Sunday school was all too much to bear. And, of course, there was the ceremonial handing out of flowers to all the moms on their way out of church. That was excruciating. Either I didn't get a flower because I wasn't a mom or someone would give me one because they felt sorry for me. Then it would end up in the trash because I refused to take it home and listen to it scream, "You're not a mother"!! Such a simple and innocent gesture would send my self- esteem spiraling downward. I may as well wear a big sign with blinking lights that says, "Barren. Can not bear children." I was not going to put myself in a situation that would be painful and sad, so it was best to just avoid any festivities.

Christmas was another holiday that I needed to let people know was painful. I, of course, could not sit at home and boycott Christmas. My family would've had me committed. But I could help them to realize that there were aspects of Christmas that I tried to avoid such as going to the malls. Why? Because they were filled with kids and families and the focus was the chubby old man wearing a red suit with a line of kids all waiting anxiously to give him their list of toys and all the parents waiting for the treasured photo. Malls were a no-no for me. Actually, I tried to steer clear of any public arena and all of those warm fuzzy family moments. The children's Christmas program at church bore a huge red flag. Finding a Christmas card in the mailbox was something I feared. The card most certainly contained a happy picture of the family sending warm wishes, a cute picture of the kids in their holiday outfits or a charming letter detailing how blessed they were to have such a wonderful family and documenting all of the activities and accomplishments of their kids. Most times I didn't even open the cards. Would someone not dealing personally with infertility think receiving Christmas cards would be painful? Probably not. That is why I so liked the idea of sending this letter. It informed my friends of some of the daily struggles and simple things that could push me over the edge. I didn't get much response from people after I sent them. I don't know if they appreciated my thoughts and read it with open hearts or if it confirmed to them that I was losing it. But I felt better, and I had accomplished my goal.

13
THE SEARCH FOR HELP

I had had three miscarriages now. (One loss had been a tubal pregnancy.) I didn't know where to go from there. Obviously something was wrong somewhere even if the doctors couldn't find what it was. I wanted so desperately for a doctor to say, "Here is the problem and here is how it can be fixed." But that wasn't happening. I didn't think I was willing to try again to get pregnant. It was too exhausting and hard. I didn't want to invest money and emotion in fertility treatments only to have false hope and then be let down yet again. I was so lost. I dreamed of having a baby with Bill, to be able to look into the baby's face and see the reflection of Bill. I wanted to be pregnant. I wanted to have morning sickness. I wanted to have the amazing experience of feeling a child growing inside of me and, as crazy as it sounds, I wanted to feel the pain of giving birth. I longed for monthly doctor visits and buying maternity clothes and measuring my growing belly and everything that goes along with it, good and bad. I wanted to give my husband, the man I adored and loved with all my heart, a child. I was heartbroken to think that may never happen. I felt incomplete as a woman and as a wife. I was grieving the loss of a fourth baby and the death of a dream--a dream that I had worked so hard to try to fill.

I also felt very abandoned by God. Why wasn't He listening to my prayers? Was I being punished for something? Why had He put the desire in my heart to be a mother if He wasn't going to give me a child?

I felt as if He was dangling a carrot in front of me--teasing--only to rip it away and leave me wanting it even more. Were we supposed to give up? Throw in the towel? Did we go through all of this for nothing? Were the four losses obvious signs from God that it was not in His plan for us to be parents, and we weren't willing to see it? Was I ever going to be okay again? Were we supposed to adopt? I had so many questions and no answers. I did know one thing. I had to find something to give me hope. I had to find something to cling to that would have a happy ending. And I knew I needed professional help.

I had no idea where to go for that help. Decision making was certainly not my strong suit at that point in the journey. The thought of having to find a therapist who was able to help me sort through all of my issues, who maybe had experienced pregnancy losses or dealt with infertility herself, and who was covered by our insurance was all very overwhelming. Money shouldn't have been an issue. My mental and emotional health and ability to function and carry on should take the front seat. But money was an issue. Therapists are expensive, especially when you have no idea how often or for how long you're going to need to see one. So, I was limited as to who was on our mental health plan. I don't know if it was me or Bill, probably Bill, who suggested the therapist that Bill's mother had seen for years to help her with her depression and the issues that she had. Linda had really liked her and had thought a lot of her. I didn't know anything about her, but it was a connection. It was better than simply picking a name out of an insurance directory. I don't remember the specifics of how we found where she was working so that I could contact her. Looking back now, I know it was God's direction. I gave her a call and told her who I was and asked if she would accept my insurance. Again, I don't remember all the details. I know there were a few hoops I had to jump through to be covered, but in the end, God brought me to her and allowed me to see her for a time.

I was very excited and very nervous before my first visit with the therapist. I was excited because I was finally going to get help dealing with all the crappy feelings I had. I was bringing in the big guns…someone who hopefully knew how to fix me. There was a small chance maybe I could work through all of this and become myself again. I missed the old me. I desperately wanted her back. She was hidden somewhere deep in a pit beneath the pain and grief and the identity of infertility. There was hope I would be able to dig through the layers of rubble and bring her back to life again. I had someone now who would be able to reach down and help me out. I was nervous because I hoped I hadn't forgotten how to be myself. When I did crawl out of the dark and lonely pit, when I finally saw that first beam of sunlight on my face and felt the warmth of the hope it brings, when I could dust all the dirt and grime off and stand up straight again...would I know what to do? I had been at the bottom of this pit for so long. Miserable or not, it had become my home. I had hung my hat, decorated with tears, and furnished it with anger and grief. It was what I knew. It was familiar. I knew how to be sad and how to feel isolated and hopeless. I expected the dirt to keep piling in on top of me forever and to keep covering me with fear and guilt and emptiness and confusion and resentment. Even though these were not things I wanted, they had become a part of me. It was scary to think of removing them. What would be left? Would I still be the girl that Bill had fallen in love with? Would he still want me? I had been covered by the dirt for so long, it had become part of my skin. If I washed the dirt away, would part of the old healthy skin wash away too? It was scary to begin the process of emerging from this pit, but I knew it had to be done. I had no choice if I wanted to live again.

My first visit was April 16, 2004. I was a little nervous while waiting in the office. I tried to thumb through a magazine, but I couldn't concentrate, even on that. I saw several patients come in and several more leave. I wondered what their stories were. Were they as messed up as I felt? How long had they been coming to see a therapist? Did they really need help or did they just like talking about themselves every week? Was I going to become a person who depended on a therapist to get through life? Would she hear my story and think there's hope for me or will she call the men in white coats to take me away because I'm beyond hope?

Our first meeting went very well and very fast. Her office was small and intimate and decorated with dark cherry furniture that I love. It was in the basement of the building, so natural light was straining to peek through the tiny window. There was a lamp that helped light the room, but it had that warm, cozy, soft, comfortable feel. I sat on a small couch and she sat across from me in a big chair. It wasn't at all like I had envisioned from seeing movies. We spent the first ten or fifteen minutes talking about Linda. She had passed away just a few months before. It had been a while since Linda had seen her, and so I filled her in with the basics. Then I began recounting the events of the past three years. I shared the facts of my four pregnancies and the emotional turmoil they left in their wake. I cried, and she listened. She was an excellent listener. I knew she was getting paid to listen to me, but I didn't care. She seemed genuinely concerned and interested in me. There hadn't been many people in my life who were willing just to sit and listen. She asked questions to help her understand where I was and clarify some facts and the timeline of events. There was really never any quiet time. If I was upset and not able to talk, she would tell a little about herself and that she too, was infertile--an answered prayer. What a blessing to be talking to a therapist who knew my pain first-hand. She had never experienced a pregnancy loss, but she knew the pain of not being able to have a child while everyone else was doing it with such ease. She knew some of my heartache. The time was spent giving her the big picture, so we didn't have time to focus on one issue or emotion. Lately, every hour always seemed to crawl by, but this hour flew! We ended our hour session, and she walked me back to the waiting area. I felt great! I had taken the first step toward feeling sunlight again, and I could hardly wait to come back and start digging my way out!

During our first meeting, my therapist told me that she had adopted three children. She wasn't able to get pregnant, so she and her husband chose a different route to become parents. Adoption. The word had been mentioned a time or two over the past year, but never with any seriousness. It was something we knew was out there, but never put much thought into. I had been thinking a little more about it lately, but was afraid to say it out loud to Bill. That would be an admission of failure on my part. I would be admitting that I couldn't do it. I couldn't conceive a child and carry it to term. I couldn't give Bill a baby that was the reflection of us and a product of our love. I couldn't do what every other woman on the face of the earth could do. I couldn't do what my body was supposed to do.

I couldn't give up. What if the next pregnancy would be successful? I couldn't give up on our baby.

Here is my journal entry from April 17, 2004:

Adoption is so scary to me right now. I feel like it's our only option, but I have hesitations. And the process scares me-people looking at our lives under a magnifying glass--someone else deciding if we get to be parents. I don't know if I'm ready mentally or emotionally to face all that is involved. I just don't know what to do. Should I get a job and focus on that for awhile? But I don't want to wait too long-if we start pushing forty, it may take longer to get a baby if we decide to adopt. I feel guilty for wanting to give up on having our own baby. What if the next pregnancy should be successful? This is just all too hard. It's supposed to be easy and happy. I'm tired of this heavy black cloud hanging over us. There are no easy answers and how are we supposed to know the right answer?

During this time period when I was seeing the therapist, I kept going to my volunteer job at the hospital. I still liked having an escape from my life for a few hours each week. However, my job at the front desk was proving to be a little tough on me emotionally. The information desk was right inside the front doors and so I had a front row seat to all of the expectant mothers and fathers coming in and also to all of the new mommies being wheeled out of the hospital with their tiny, wonderful new bundles of joy on their laps. I saw all of the nervous fathers bringing in the car seats and all of the big shiny "It's A Boy" or "It's A Girl" balloons whooshing by. I had to give room numbers and directions to all of the excited family members and friends who came to see the little miracle and I had to endure stories about the labor and the reward. I had to watch the dads drive up in the cars and load them up with flowers and gifts and then, of course, watch as the happy couple placed their newborn in the car for the first time. Grandma and grandpa were sometimes there to catch the whole scene on video and take pictures. Everyone would be smiling from ear to ear and the happiness would be oozing from every direction. Only when the oozing got to me, I would feel sick to my stomach. It was torture to have to watch these scenes unfold and feel my empty, broken womb ache. I needed to find a different job in a different place where I didn't have to watch these horrendous moments. I also remember one afternoon at the information desk when I saw a very pregnant young girl, IV in tow, walk outside the front doors and light up a cigarette. I couldn't believe what I was seeing! It took every bit of restraint I had not to walk right up to her and give her a good hard slap. I had tried everything in my power to have a healthy pregnancy and to give my babies everything they needed to be healthy and thrive. Here this girl was taking her baby's health for granted or not caring if her baby was healthy. It was something I didn't want to see again. So I transferred to a job on the second floor doing paperwork. I was tucked away in a back corner and didn't have to come face-to-face with all of the baby hoopla. It was a good move. There was so much work to do. I hardly had time to breathe for the four or five hours I was there. I could immerse myself in filing and mundane work that didn't allow any time for my mind to rest and then to wander, unlike working at the information desk. I liked meeting the people and offering a helpful hand, but there were times when no one stopped by the desk and the clock ticked by so slowly. That was the way for me all the time. The clock seemed to tick more slowly the past few years. Each day passing as agonizingly and pain-stakingly slow as the next.

I was encouraged by my weekly therapy sessions. My second session I remember well. We had covered the basics in the first initial session. Now it was time to start focusing on specific issues. I remember telling her about how I just wanted to "cocoon"-to stay at home and not have to be around people or be in social situations. I didn't know if that was a healthy and o.k. thing to do because everyone around me was trying to scoot me out the door and push me into the big scary world that I didn't feel ready to face. She gave me permission to cocoon. It felt so good to hear someone say, "It's o.k. to stay inside where you're comfortable and can be yourself. It's o.k. to let yourself be sad. You can't feel better because someone tells you that you should." She told me that I am in control of the timetable for my feelings and emotions. No one else should be trying to dictate that timetable. What a relief! She gave me the confidence to let people know that I was going to heal as slowly as I needed to and that I shouldn't feel pressured by anyone to do anything I didn't feel I was ready for. It was a big step.

She also helped me realize that what I was feeling-- the grief, and pain, and guilt-- was normal and expected for my situation. I shouldn't expect myself to just bounce back and recover from the journey I had been on. It was going to take time, but I was on the right path. I was headed in the right direction and I had someone to walk beside me. It was amazing how quickly I seemed to turn the corner. Being able to talk with her each week and having her validate my feelings meant so much. She helped me face my demons, so to speak. She helped me be real and true and deal with the nasty emotions I had for so long tried to ignore. I truly believe that is what God placed in my life that helped me move on. I had finally faced the so unpleasant task of bringing to the surface all of the feelings that I didn't want to admit I had that were weighing me down and not allowing me to climb out of the slimy, slippery pit. Once I brought them to the surface, faced them, and dealt with them, I could let them go and begin the journey of climbing out. Oh how amazing it felt to be rid of that weight! To be able to be free and honest with myself and finally able to see the rays of sunlight breaking through the mud and grime!

"Therefore we do not lose heart. Though outwardly we are wasting away, yet inwardly we are being renewed day by day. For our light and momentary troubles are achieving for us an eternal glory that far outweighs them all. So we fix our eyes not on what is seen, but on what is unseen. For what is seen is temporary, but what is unseen is eternal." 2 Corinthians 4:16-18

14
ADOPTION?

It was amazing how quickly adoption changed from being a scary and almost forbidden word to a word that flowed more easily. Adoption. Adoption. Adoption. I could at least speak it out loud and could allow it to creep more closely to my forethoughts.

So Bill and I began to talk more seriously about the idea. I really needed something positive and hopeful to cling to, something that would have a happy ending, even if it took a while. Bill was a little reserved about the idea. The media only tells of the failed adoptions, cases where the birthparents come and rip the child away when he is two years old. That was all we really knew about it, what the media chose to show us. He viewed adoption as scary and risky. What if that happens to us? We thought we had seen hard times, but nothing we had been through would compare to the pain of an adoption going sour. I understood his fears, and I shared them. He was also hesitant because of possibly not knowing any medical or emotional history of an adopted child, the "not knowing what you're going to get" fear. I understood that as well, but it wasn't as much of a concern to me as it was to him. I figured when you have a biological child, you still "don't know what you're going to get." Granted, you have a knowledge of family history, but there are still a million things that aren't hereditary. I think one of Bill's fears was that the child would grow up to be violent or a thief or a murderer. I don't think anyone has any guarantees that their child will grow up to be healthy, well adjusted, and stable. I do believe that the environment that the child grows up in plays a huge role in that, though. I am certainly not a psychiatrist or a sociologist, but I can't help but feel strongly that if a child is surrounded by love from both parents and feels accepted and valued and knows the importance of discipline and boundaries, that's an enormous determining factor in his mental and social well being. All we can do as parents is raise them and teach the best we know how. The rest is a matter of prayer no matter if the child is biological or adopted.

We both have quite a few medical issues in our family's histories, from diabetes to heart problems to depression. A biological child would possibly inherit all of these things. So we didn't see an adopted child being any different. He would inherit the same or similar conditions, just not from us. There was no guarantee if we had a biological child, that he would be born perfectly healthy with no concerns or problems. There would be a guarantee, though, if I were pregnant, that our child would not be born addicted to drugs or alcohol. That is what we wanted for our baby, biological or adopted.

I began researching adoption as much as I could-- buying books, searching the Web, visiting the library, talking to people, going to seminars and calling agencies.

Bill and I went to our first information meeting at an adoption agency in June of 2004, only three months after my last miscarriage. I was surprised at how quickly adoption went from being a scary word that I couldn't even manage to mutter out loud to a word that I was excited about. I was excited about finally having something positive to cling to and a hope of finally being able to be a mother. I wanted to know everything there was to know about adoption. I was ready to begin a different journey.

And this was indeed a different journey. The journey of infertility that we had been on was a long and weary one that had brought us to the desert and left us stranded. The thought of traveling again on another journey was scary. We were tired. Did we have the strength and energy left to begin a new journey that we knew nothing about? We were going to be traveling into unfamiliar territory. We knew about infertility. Bill once commented that he knew more about a uterus than he ever wanted to know. I felt the same way. Now we were going to have to forget all of that information and begin learning new information. But I felt energized and ready to start down the road that would lead us to a child.

There was a lot to learn. With infertility, you learn as you go. The information comes on a need to know basis. There's not much reason to learn about in vitro unless you've tried everything else and that's your last effort. With adoption, you learn everything up front. We knew we wanted to apply for a domestic adoption, not an international one, so that cut down a little on the information needed. But I was still overwhelmed at all of the hoops we had to go through. And that became an area where I developed a fairly hefty amount of bitterness and anger. I couldn't believe all the things they (meaning the agency and the state) were requiring us to do to POSSIBLY become parents. Did they not know all of the crap we had already been through? Hadn't our past three year journey through hell and back proven us to be worthy and deserving? We had suffered so much and now we had to suffer through the humiliation of having our lives looked at under a magnifying glass by people we had never met. A complete stranger sitting behind a desk somewhere was going to review all of our paperwork and decide if we were fit to be someone's parents. Even today, I feel a bit of bitterness towards this whole aspect of the process. If it's so critical for a home with a baby to have a fire extinguisher and an evacuation plan, why doesn't the state require it of ALL homes and parents? Anyway...

15
A NEW JOURNEY

We decided to get on a waiting list at a local adoption agency. Several people had asked us over the past few years why we didn't give up on having a biological child and just adopt, like it was that simple and easy. It was very scary to start on a new journey, to have to leave everything familiar, even if it was painful, and travel into the unknown. It took a great deal of emotional strength to begin thinking a different way and having to learn new information. It also took a great deal of spiritual strength to decide to go in a new direction. There was no burning bush. Oh! How I had longed for a burning bush! Please Lord, let me hear Your voice and tell us what You would have us do. But we had to simply rely on our faith and our heart and trust that we were following God's direction and guidance. It was not a decision that was made overnight or made easily. It was exhausting and deflating. But once the decision was made, it was exciting to think of the possibility! We were required to complete a home study, which included all of the hoops and paperwork and then some, and also to complete a few classes about adoption and infant care. Again, I was a little bitter and resentful of all we had to do, but I felt we were on the right path.

We began the task of filling out papers and making copies of financial records and making appointments for the fire inspector to come. We had to take an infant CPR class and have a criminal background check done, which included getting fingerprinted. We had to go downtown to the criminal justice center to have that done. We had to stand in line next to people waiting to see their loved ones or friends who were in jail. I felt like a criminal. When it came our turn at the window to pay, I felt it necessary to tell the officer why we were there. I also felt it necessary to tell the officer who actually took our prints. They didn't care. But I needed to make sure they knew I was a law abiding citizen and simply trying to have a baby.

Even though I resented having to go through all of the hoops and do all of the paperwork, at least I felt like I was actively involved in the process. I was good at making lists, getting the jobs done, and then marking them off the list. At least I had a job, something I could contribute, something I could succeed at. I felt I was in control, at least to some extent with the process. I could make sure things were done and done on time. And there was the small flicker of hope. I had taken all of my eggs out of one basket and put them into another, so to speak. We were taking a different approach-- an approach that had a better chance of having a happy ending, an approach that would hopefully lead to me becoming a mother. So I took on the task of going through hoop after hoop and marking things off my list. I was feeling more and more encouraged and excited and hopeful.

The home study also included being interviewed by one of the agency's social workers. I had to be interviewed by myself, Bill by himself, and then the two of us interrogated--I mean interviewed--together. This part of the process was very difficult for me. I couldn't believe we had to endure the questions and probing after all we had been through. Hadn't our journey proven that we wanted a child from the bottom of our broken hearts? People don't go through all of that just for fun. But, we had to do it, so I sucked it up and answered all of the stupid questions. Why do you want to be parents? What was your childhood like? Of course I had a sarcastic answer for each of the questions that I had to hold back. I did tell the social worker at the beginning of my interview how I felt about this portion of the home study. They told us to be honest in our answers, so I felt I should be honest about how I felt about the questions. She seemed to respect my feelings and understood it was difficult for me. We survived and apparently answered everything to their satisfaction because we were "approved" at the beginning of December 2004. The work and the lists had been completed. Now we had to wait. And wait. And wait.

When we were added to the agency's waiting list, we had to fill out a form asking a hundred different questions about what type of baby we were willing to adopt--the sex, age, race, and a thousand different medical conditions. We felt very strongly that we wanted a caucasian newborn that didn't have alcohol or drug addictions. Some people looked down on us for this decision. I guess they figured since we had tried so long to have a family and were "desperate," we should just take whatever comes along and be grateful. But we wanted a newborn. We wanted to be a part of our child's life from day one. We didn't want to miss anything. We wanted a caucasian baby. That's what we were. That's what we knew. We wanted a baby not born with addictions. That's what I would be able to provide my own biological child. I could not guarantee a healthy child of my own, but I could guarantee I wouldn't smoke, drink, or do drugs. This was going to be our child forever and this was what we wanted for our family, selfish or not. We were the ones that were going to have to live with what we chose, not anyone else. I did not appreciate the feeling we received from a few people when they found out what we had indicated for our choices. We also knew that the wait was longer the more specific you were with race and medical conditions, like addictions. We were willing to wait.

Adoption has changed a great deal over the past few decades. It used to be if a birth mother decided to place her baby for adoption, she was lucky to even see the baby or know the sex before it was whisked away. She rarely was given the chance to hold her new baby. And chances were she did not know who was adopting her child or know anything about them. A nurse simply took the baby away and that was that. She was left wondering for the rest of her life sometimes what ever happened to her child and if he was happy and loved.

Not so today. From what I understand of adoption, it is rare that a mother places a baby unless she knows about the couple, maybe even meets them before the baby is born, and the adoptive parents agree to some form of openness. She is in total control of who her baby is placed with. She wants to be the one picking the family, not the agency. So we were required to put together a profile of ourselves for the adoption agency. It was basically our story of who we were, what kind of life we had, and a little about our hopes and dreams for our family and our future child. It was a small, general, non-identifying glimpse into our lives. These profiles were kept on file and then shown to a prospective birthmother if the agency thought we would make a good match for what the birthmother was looking for. We thought this would be a simple and easy assignment. No. Basically what we were asked to do was to create a booklet to sell ourselves to a birthmother. She could possibly be shown several profiles and, of course, our ultimate goal was for her to choose us. So we needed our profile to convince the birth mom that we were the best choice, without making it look obvious that we were trying to sell ourselves. Easier said than done. We analyzed and labored over every sentence we wrote. We didn't want to sound too desperate and needy. Nor did we want to come across as too perfect and unrealistic. What should we include? How much was too much information? It was a struggle. We had no idea what a birth mother may be looking for. A counselor from the adoption agency told us during one of our classes that you never know what a birth mother may be looking for. It may be something as simple as the couple takes a vacation every year, or they have a pet, or they like music. Her point was that you just had to be honest and real and trust that the right birth mom would be led to your profile. I was so relieved when we finally had it finished. We had to trust that God would match us up with the right birth mom.

During the adoption journey, I was finally able to let go of the ugly beast called control. I had been fighting this battle for four years now. I'm not a control "freak" by any means, but during all of the pregnancy trials and losses, I felt completely out of control. I was certainly not in control of my body. I was not in control of the doctors. I was not in control of my feelings. I was not in control of other people and their responses to me. I felt very much like I was spiraling OUT of control, never again being able to regain it. So I clung to any thread of control that I could find. I didn't want to admit that I didn't have control, at all, over becoming parents. I would only reveal to people what I wanted them to see as a way of having some control. I wasn't able to give it all to God 100%. I could only give 95% and then hold on to that little 5% that was left. I needed to have a say and a voice in what happened. I trusted God, but I was going to help Him. I was saying, "Here God--You can have this, but I'm going to keep hold of this little corner to be sure it's done the way I want." And God said, "No, child. You must give it all to me and trust that I know what's best for you." That's a hard thing to do! There is a saying that's quite popular in the church world that simply says "Let go and let God". That is *so* easy to say and *so* difficult to do. There is no handbook on how to accomplish that feat. No one can tell you ten simple steps to letting go. It is a matter of your heart and attitude and faith. It took me four years of God whispering in my ear before I relented and said,

"Okay Lord. I can't do this. I'm tired and I'm weary. I give this ALL to You, every last piece." It was amazing how quickly my spirit began to heal. It was freedom that I hadn't known before. There had not been a time in my life when I had been completely able to let go. I had learned that even if I think I am in control, I am not. God's plan and His purpose is so much bigger than I can imagine.

The next several months were fairly uneventful. We did start preparing the nursery. We painted the room and borrowed the crib from my sister. We began thinking of names. We were hopeful and excited. I called the agency every month to check and see if our profile had been shown to anyone. It hadn't, but that didn't dampen our spirits. We knew that God brought the right babies into the right families. In one of our classes at the agency, we met a couple who was trying to be approved quickly because they already had a baby in their home. It was a friend of a friend situation. They had the baby and had agreed to adopt him, but did not have any claim or legal custody of him. So, needless to say, they were in a hurry to get things done. At first, their situation made us angry. They had not asked for this child. They actually had three children of their own already. This had just been dropped in their lap. We resented the fact that we had tried so hard and been through so much and then this family just had a baby dropped off at their door step, so to speak. It was very unfair. But the more we talked with them and got to know them, the more we realized that baby was supposed to be with them. He looked exactly like the adoptive father with his dark eyes and hair and Cuban complexion. There was a possibility that he could have some drug addiction issues as he got older and they were willing to work through that. They were also willing to take the baby into their home and hearts without any legal authority at all. He was supposed to be with them. He fit. That situation, along with other stories we had heard, solidified the fact for us that God would bring the right baby and the right birth mother into our lives at just the right time. And He did.

16
THE PHONE CALL

It was a Thursday morning, June 9, 2005, four years to the day since my first surgery and my journey into the depths of despair. I was getting ready to leave the house for my volunteer shift at the hospital. I was ready to walk out the door when the phone rang. Normally, I would've let the answering machine get it. I wouldn't want to be late. But that morning I answered the phone. It was God's prodding.

"Is this Sandy Hickman?" the voice asked.

"It is."

"Are you and your husband still wanting to adopt?" he asked.

"Yes," I answered a little hesitantly.

"I am a lawyer (he gave his name) and I have a client who is wanting to place her baby and she was given your name."

My head began to swim. What? What did he say? Did he say what I think he said? I needed to answer him.

"Okay." That was all I could come up with. I needed to ask more questions.

"Who is your client? How did she get our name?" I asked.

"Let's just say she's a friend of a friend." was his reply.

My mind immediately starting going through all of my friends trying to think of someone who knew someone who was pregnant. My mind was blank.

The conversation continued, and I discovered a little more information. It was a teenage girl who went to the same church as my sister. I remember my sister telling me about her a while ago when she first found out she was pregnant, but she had said she thought she was going to keep the baby. This girl wanted to see our profile.

"Would you be able to drop off your profile this afternoon?" the lawyer asked.

"You bet your britches I would!!" I'm sure I said it a little nicer, but I would've driven our profile to California at that point if she wanted to see it.

When I hung up the phone, I called Bill at work right away. I'm not sure what I told him. I'm sure his head was swimming too. I didn't really know very much except that our prayers were about to be answered.

I also called my sister on her cell phone. She was out shopping. I told her I had just received a phone call from a lawyer wanting to know if we were still interested in adopting. She didn't seem surprised.

"You did?" she answered a bit sheepishly.

So I told her what I knew and asked if she knew anymore.

She then told me the story of how a few months ago she was in a Bible study with the young girl's mother and how she had told the group that her sister and her

123

husband were on a waiting list to adopt and requested prayer for us. The teen's mother came up to Patti after the study and asked her a few questions about us like if we were Christians and a few more basic questions. Patti told her that she didn't want to get involved and set up any false hopes for us. We had been through enough. If her daughter was really serious about placing, she needed to contact our adoption agency. That had been the end of it. Patti did not say anything to us about the possibility. I have to give her credit for being disciplined and restrained! How she kept it to herself, I'll never know.

So now I was on my way to give our profile to this young girl. I felt a peace. I truly believed from the time I hung up from talking with the lawyer that this was going to be <u>our</u> baby. I felt like our long journey that we had started out on five years ago was about to come to an end--a happy end.

I dropped off our profile at the home where she was living at the time. It was a home for pregnant teenage girls that a church in our area ran. It was a beautiful place. I dropped off the book at the information desk and headed back home. Not long after I returned home, the lawyer called again and said that the girl wanted to meet us in person the following day at the home if that was possible. Again, I would've gone to the moon and back doing somersaults the whole way, but I simply said yes.

Her name was Sam. She was due in four weeks. Four weeks! To everyone else, that seemed like no time at all to prepare and get ready. To us, it seemed like an eternity. We had been prepared for years. I just wanted the journey to be over and to be a mom and to get on with being a family. Four weeks seemed like four years.

Bill left work early that Friday so that we could meet her in the afternoon. It was about an hour drive to the home and, of course, traffic was thick. I was anxious to see her and worried we were going to be late and make a bad impression. There was nothing I could do about it. As I've said earlier in the book, music was and still is important to me. It speaks to me and the lyrics often seem to be written just for me. That day the sky was dark and cloudy, and it had been raining. We were creeping along the highway in silence, each of us a million miles away with our own thoughts, when the sun began to sneak through those dark clouds. I could see rays of sunshine streaming down among the dark gloomy clouds. The song, "I Can See Clearly Now" by Johnny Nash came on the radio. It was an old song from the 70's that I had always liked and enjoyed singing along to, but it never meant much to me. All that changed during the course of the song that day. The words grabbed my heart and brought tears to me eyes. Yes! I was out of the pit. I had emerged from the grime and the heavy weight of the soil of despair and pain and hopelessness. I could finally feel the warmth of the sun on my skin and my eyes were blinking and straining to adjust to the brightness.

I can see clearly now the rain is gone/ I can see all obstacles in my way/

Gone are the dark clouds that had me blind/It's gonna be a bright bright sun shiny day

I again felt a sense of calm and assuredness that God had His hand on us and that He was about to bless us beyond our imagination.

Sam recognized me right away. She said I looked just like my sister. I wasn't sure how to greet her. Should I shake her hand? Should I hug her? I think I just said hello and made some silly small talk. Sam's social worker from the home was there with her and so was her mother, Betty, and stepfather. The social worker showed us into a large comfy room where we sat down. Sam had some questions for us that weren't answered in our profile. I tried to stay calm and not show how nervous I was. This was the most important interview of our lives! We had been told from the classes at the agency to try to answer questions from a birth mother as honestly as possible. You don't know what kind of answers she's looking for, so all you can do is give your best and be yourselves. God will take care of the rest. One thing we had learned was that God was in control. So we had approached the meeting with that attitude. We believed it really didn't matter what we said if God's plan was for this child to be a part of our family. He would provide, and if it was meant to be, it would happen.

Sam's first question to us was, "Do you want a boy or a girl?" We answered it didn't matter. She replied quickly with, "Well, I'm having a boy." Okay then. We knew right away she was going to be a girl who spoke what was on her mind without hesitation. We were happy to hear it was a boy. I wanted Bill to have a son. It of course didn't matter to us, but if we would've had the chance to choose, we would've both chosen a boy. She went on to ask more of her list of questions.

"Why do you want a child?"

"How strong is your faith?"

"Are you open to an open adoption?"

"What would he call me?"

"What's a lesson you've learned from your parents?"

"Do you have a name picked out?"

"Would you ever go back to teaching?"

"Would you home school?"

"Where have you traveled?"

"Do you smoke?"

"How long have you wanted a child?"

We answered all of her questions as best we could. I choked up a few times when talking about our faith and how long we had wanted a child. We seemed to be on the same page as far as openness and expectations. Sam was only seventeen and didn't feel ready emotionally or financially to take care of a baby. She still had a year of high school to finish. The father was not in the picture so she would not have his help and support. It just felt right. I had always dreaded meeting with a birth mother when our time came. I was so afraid it would be awkward and commercial, like we were applying for a job, not simply wanting to be responsible and to love a baby. But it didn't feel awkward at all. It felt comfortable and peaceful.

After Sam had finished asking her questions, the social worker from the home told us Sam would take a few days to think about things, but Sam piped up and interrupted and said, "I don't need a few days. I know I want them." It was such a relief to hear. I think there were possibly trumpets playing in the background and a choir singing the "Hallelujah Chorus". We talked for a few more minutes before saying goodbye. I gave her a hug and whispered thank you in her ear. When Bill and I walked outside, the sun was shining and we grabbed each other and hugged and cried and whispered to each other that we were finally going to be parents. We flew home on a cloud accompanied by violins and harps.

My friend from college that I had gone to visit with my first pregnancy was in town that weekend and we had planned to get together that night. After we left the home, I called her to tell her the good news. Her response was "let's go register for baby stuff!!!" She was so excited for us. So we met for dinner and then headed to the baby superstore and had a great time looking at all of the baby necessities and extras. She had three children so she knew the practical side of all the "must haves", what worked and what didn't. She was a terrific help to me that night in helping to pick out baby items and for simply sharing my excitement.

The next four weeks raced by and drug by simultaneously. This was it! This was going to be the last time for a long while that it would be just me and Bill. That made me a little sad. I wanted to cherish every last second the two of us had together. Our life we had had for thirteen years was about to change forever. Even though we were ready and had been waiting for this moment so long, it was still a little scary. I wondered if I would miss all the time we spent together by ourselves. I wondered if

I would be jealous of Bill wanting to spend time with the baby instead of me. I also had those initial fears from the very beginning of our talk of adoption about being able to love a child that we did not create. Would I be able to love him right away? I hadn't had nine months to fall in love--only a few weeks. But then I had loved our four babies that we had lost so very early in my pregnancies. But those were OUR children, made by the love that we had for one another. This was different. What if I didn't feel love or feel connected to this baby? All of these thoughts and concerns made the weeks go by fast. There was a very tiny part of me that dreaded the end of our time with just each other and having to face the answers to my questions.

But we were so eager to see our child! I had dreamed of this day for the past five years, when we first began trying for a family. Oh how my arms had ached to be able to hold our baby and look into his eyes and tell him I loved him. Our journey was coming to an end, and I wanted it so much to be over. I spent a lot of time in the nursery making sure every little detail was taken care of. I washed all of the clothes we had been given and that we had bought. I registered at the local baby store and had a wonderful time picking out items for my want list. I helped my sister plan our baby shower and we put the infant seat in the car. We were ready. We just needed the baby. The days went by at a snail's pace. Sam was young, and this was her first baby. I had heard that this scenario sometimes leads to early delivery. I kept my cell phone literally in my hand all the time. I didn't want to miss a phone call saying she was in labor. The days crept along.

I met with Sam two more times during those few weeks. Bill and I went to visit with her again about a week or so after our first meeting. We sat and talked with her for about an hour. We talked mostly about superficial things. I really don't remember the conversation. Then I went by myself one afternoon and had lunch with Sam and her mom and step dad. Bill had to work. I could tell it was hard for her mom to know that Sam wasn't able to keep her first grandchild. I tried not to show too much excitement, to respect their feelings and their situation. At the same time, we had learned in our adoption classes that birth mothers want you to be excited about the baby. They want to know that the baby is going to be a happy and welcomed addition to the family. That was difficult and awkward for me, trying to find a balance in my excitement and enthusiasm. We discussed the nursery that day and plans that Bill and I were making to get ready. We also discussed me being in the delivery room when the baby was born. I was thrilled! I was eager to be able to share those first precious moments with our child and very grateful that Sam would allow me that privilege. She also asked if Bill would want to cut the umbilical cord. Again, I was surprised and delighted at how involved she seemed comfortable with us being. Bill does not do well with medical procedures and blood, so I left that offer unanswered.

Sam's due date was July 6, 2005. She had a doctor's appointment on the sixth. That afternoon, Sam's social worker called me to tell me that the doctor was going to do a cesarean section the following morning. Sam is a small girl and he was afraid the baby was going to be too big to deliver vaginally. I was ecstatic! She also told me that Sam's mom did not want us at the hospital until after the baby was born and Sam was settled. We were very disappointed--especially me. I would not be able now to see my son born and be one of the first people to hold him and be a part of those first hours. I was angry at her mom. I knew in my heart that Sam didn't care if we were there, but that her mom was the one calling the shots. I felt like I was being robbed of something I had a right to, even though I knew in adoption situations that you're lucky to be able to be involved in the birth. When my son was older and asked me about the day he was born, I wanted to be able to tell him every detail about his birth and now I was not going to have all of the information. I had to remind myself that I had no rights at all to this child until Sam signed the papers, which she couldn't sign until seventy-two hours after the birth, so until that time, I had to be gracious and grateful for what they gave us. That evening, Bill and I went to one of our favorite restaurants on the river and then went to a park overlooking the river and talked and enjoyed our last evening together. It was a beautiful night.

I didn't sleep at all. Sam's c-section was scheduled for 8 a.m. I finally got out of bed around seven. I turned the television on to help pass the time. There had been bombings in England's subway that morning, so I immersed myself in the news trying to not think about what I was missing at the hospital. I wrote our son a letter while sitting on the couch. I told him how I was waiting to hear that he had been born and how much we loved him and couldn't wait to hold and see him. I told him all that I wished for him in life and how God had brought us together to be a family. When he is older and understands that he is adopted and understands what that means, I want to be able to share with him this amazing journey and help him to see how God worked in our lives and in Sam's to bring him into our hearts.

Bill and I found it impossible to sit at home that morning waiting for the phone to ring. We decided to go ahead and leave to take our dog to my parent's house. They were going to keep her for a few days until we brought the baby home and got into a routine. I was beginning to worry a little because I had asked Betty to at least call us when the baby was born to let us know everything was okay. I had expected to hear from her at least by ten that morning and it was now almost eleven. Every minute felt like an hour. Finally, a little after eleven, Sam's step dad called my cell phone to tell us the baby had been born, he was healthy, Sam was doing fine, and we could come on to the hospital. We kissed my mom and dad and ran out the door to go meet our son.

When we arrived at the hospital, we stopped by the nurse's station and told them who we were. The nurse gave me a bracelet that would allow me to see the baby whenever I wanted. I felt like I was in a dream. We went to see Sam first to check on her and take her some flowers we had brought. She was still in the recovery room. We spent a few minutes with her and then the nurse came to take us to the nursery. Sam told us, "Go enjoy your son."

I was hoping Betty and her step dad were still at lunch. I was still angry at her for taking away sharing in the birth, and I really didn't want to see her. We had given them their time and now I wanted ours. But they were in the nursery, and she was holding the baby. The nurse led us to a little room off the nursery and Betty handed me my child.

17
JOSHUA GARROD HICKMAN

Joshua Garrod Hickman was born on Thursday, July 7, 2005 at 8:05a.m. He weighed 5 pounds and 15 ounces. Joshua was a name Bill and I both liked and Garrod was Bill's mother's maiden name. He was beautiful. He was perfect. As soon as Betty laid him in my arms, I fell in love. All of those fears I had melted away. I would've given my life for him right then and there. I knew this was our son and that we were meant to be together. I was crying, and it all still seemed like a dream. It was so hard to believe that he was here in my arms. All we had been through--the pain, and heartache, and suffering it was all leading up to this very moment. I would have gone through it all again in a heartbeat to have this perfect, amazing little person in my arms. I wanted to sit and look at him forever. I didn't want this frame of time to end, but I finally handed him to Bill as I cried even more. He finally had a son! I was finally able to hand to him what I could not give to him. Seeing Bill with Josh made my heart melt even more and made me fall in love with him all over again. It's such an amazing sight to see your husband holding your newborn son. There was a time when I didn't think this was ever going to happen. I had pretty much given up on God blessing us as parents. Now I saw His plan. I could see the big picture. We were meant to be Joshua's parents.

"Every good and perfect gift is from above." James 1:17

The hospital was great to us. They had a room at the end of a hall that wasn't being used and really was not practical to wheel hospital beds in and out of, so they offered to let us stay there. So Thursday and Friday nights we stayed at the hospital. We were able to keep Josh in our room at night which was wonderful. We were able to feed him and change his diapers and dress him for his hospital pictures. It was great to be able to spend so much time with him. Sam had not signed her papers yet, so we were putting ourselves out there, but we felt it was important to bond with him as much as possible and for him to get to know us. Sam did spend some time with him. She had family and friends that visited and she requested him to be in her room during those times. It was hard for me to take Josh to her room and leave him. I wanted to be with him and hold him every second. I didn't want to share. I could tell Betty was having a very difficult time and Sam admitted on Friday afternoon that she was having the "baby blues." I didn't really know what to say to either of them except that I loved him and I would make sure that he had a happy and secure life. Betty seemed to be really concerned about Josh growing up in church. She wanted to be sure that he knew the truth of the gospel and that we would do all we could to be sure he would give his life to Jesus when he was older. I reassured her that God was the first priority in our house. Josh would go to Sunday school and church and Vacation Bible School and everything in between. She seemed satisfied and I believe she trusted in me to keep my word, but she still was not happy about the situation. She knew in her heart that this was the best decision for Sam and for Josh, but that did not make it easy for her. I felt they were both spending too much time with him, but I was in no position to share my opinion. I figured they needed the time to be able to say goodbye.

Friday night and Saturday morning were rough. Sam and Betty kept Josh in Sam's room late into the night. I walked by the room several times, and I could hear them crying. I so wanted to just take Josh and leave and go home, but, of course, I couldn't. We did finally bring Josh to our room after 11:00pm and kept him all night. About six Saturday morning, a nurse came in and told us that Sam and Betty had been crying a lot. Sam was supposed to be discharged that morning, and I just wanted them to do it and get it over. The nurse said she had talked with Betty around midnight and had reassured her that placing Josh was the right thing to do. I had prayed all night that God would send someone to help them. I knew leaving the hospital would be hard for them. Betty had called the youth minister from their church sometime during the night, and he had come and talked and prayed with them. I was glad he was there for them. I didn't know if they would want to see Josh again. I was scared.

"Cast your cares on the Lord and He will sustain you." Psalm 55:22

About 8:00 a.m., another nurse came in and said Sam wanted me alone to come to her room. I had no idea what to expect. I had started writing her a letter during the night, so I finished it quickly and walked down the long hall to her room. Her door was closed, and I stood outside of it for a long while before going in. I prayed for strength to face whatever was waiting for me on the other side of the door. When I walked in, Sam began crying. I went over and sat down on her bed next to her and hugged her. I couldn't imagine being in her shoes. I had tried for so long to have a baby, I couldn't dream of placing my baby for adoption. I could only begin to know the pain she felt. She told me she didn't know it was going to be this hard. I didn't know what to say. I gave her my letter and told her I admired her for having the strength to make this decision, to think of her baby before herself. She also needed reassured that she would be able to see Josh again. She had heard of a story of an adoptive family that made promises to the birth mother and then moved after everything was legalized and the birth mother never saw or heard from them again. I promised her that we would not move and that we would stay in touch as long as she wanted to. She would be able to be involved in some way in his life if that's what she chose. We talked and cried for about an hour. The minister was still there and he helped lighten the mood from time to time and helped with some awkward silent pauses. They did not ask to see Josh again. I was relieved.

I had so many emotions as I walked back down that hallway to the room where we had been staying and where

Bill was waiting for me. I was eager for Sam to leave and for us to take our baby home. I also imagined how empty Sam would be feeling leaving the hospital without her baby. I knew it was going to be rough for her during the weeks and months to come. I didn't think she had a very good support system to help her with her grief. I also knew her mom was having such a hard time and wondered how that would affect Sam. Sam was head strong and had a stubborn streak, but she was still only a child, not even eighteen. Her mom's actions and reactions would influence her a great deal.

We finally received the okay to leave the hospital. We were not able to leave until Sam had been discharged. Our lawyer was there to walk out with us. Sam was not going to court until the following Tuesday, and the hospital was not willing to keep Josh until then. We knew we were taking a baby home that was not legally ours, but we didn't want him to go to a foster home for three days. We wanted to continue to bond with him and have him with us. We did not expect any complications.

The ride home was surreal. I kept looking in the backseat at the infant car seat and pinching myself. There was a baby in it! He looked so small in his seat. I was floating. I thought I would be nervous and anxious knowing that it was just me and Bill now responsible for this little life who depended on us for everything. I knew the basics of taking care of a newborn, but had little to no experience. Surprisingly, I was very calm and confident. I wasn't worried at all about not knowing what to do or not being able to take care of his needs. It felt so natural and right. I was his mom and whatever happened, I would figure it out. Bill and I were a good team and we had been through rocky, uncertain times. Taking care of a two-day-old baby was going to be a piece of cake compared to what we had had to deal with. The important thing was that he was here and in our arms and hearts.

The next few days were typical of having a newborn in the house. We were getting acquainted with poopy diapers and middle of the night feedings. Josh was a good sleeper and never had any trouble taking his bottles. We were taking pictures and video and were so proud of our new addition. We did really well at staying calm and relaxed and enjoyed visits from our family and friends. One of my favorite times was when Bill was holding Joshua. The fears I had about feeling jealous were quickly put to rest. I loved when he had Josh, when they were sitting quietly together or when Bill was introducing him to Atlanta Braves baseball. There's nothing sexier than watching your husband rocking his son and singing him a lullaby.

18
THIS CAN'T BE HAPPENING!

On Tuesday morning, July 12th, we received a phone call from our lawyer that turned our world upside down and over and backwards. Our happiness and joy was ripped away from under us, and we didn't know what to say or do. Sam wasn't going to court to sign her papers. She was having a hard time and was second guessing her decision. There was a possibility that she wanted the baby back. My heart sank, and I felt sick. Bill was in the nursery with Josh. I hung up the phone and went to tell him what the lawyer had said. He tried to be positive and say it was just a bump in the road, but that it would be okay and not to worry. The life was being sucked out of me with each passing second. I found myself not being able to look at Josh or take care of him in any way. I was shutting down. I had to guard my heart. If she was going to take him back, I couldn't allow myself to get more attached and to fall more in love with him. Bill tended to him and I resorted back to my long lost friend, my bed. I wanted to sleep, to escape the pain. Bill called my sister, Patti, and she came to the house. We needed someone to help us make decisions, to just be there with us as our world began to fall apart. I decided that I could not keep Josh in the house any longer with this horrible, dark possibility looming above us. Bill called our lawyer and he gave us the phone number of a nice foster family. Bill called and explained our situation, and she gladly agreed to keep Josh as long as we needed her to.

Sam called at some point during the morning. She told Bill she wanted to talk to me. I remember holding the phone while she talked. I don't recall saying anything to her. I don't recall what she said to me.

The next hour or so was heart wrenching. My sister had agreed to take Josh to the foster home for us. Bill and I had to gather his things and prepare to say goodbye to our precious boy. Bill had held it together all morning and afternoon for me. He made the phone calls and talked to the lawyer, foster mom, the adoption agency, and even Sam. He was strong and got done what needed to be done. But after we got Joshua's things packed, he went off in the bedroom and lost it. That was hard for me to see and hear. He had tried to be so positive for us all day, but now the reality was sinking in for him. Sam was changing her mind and Joshua was leaving. I remember taking Joshua and sitting in the nursery in the rocking chair with him. I just sat and rocked him and cried. I told him how much I loved him and that I would always love him no matter what happened. I told him to trust Jesus. I told him that if Jesus meant for us to be together as a family that He would bring us back together. I kissed him and gave him to Patti. As I watched her pull out of the driveway with our heart, the last of whatever life was in me drove away too.

"God is our refuge and strength, an ever-present help in trouble." Psalm 46:1

The following day, Wednesday, we received a call from our lawyer that Sam did want Joshua back. He was going to pick Josh up at the foster home and meet Sam and her mom. I don't have the words to explain how I felt when Bill hung up the phone and told me the news. If all the sadness, desperation, heartbreak, fear, anger, and every other awful emotion I had felt for the past five years could be put all together and felt at once, it would only be a drop in the bucket of the pain I felt that moment. I began to cry and wail and yell at God. I've never cried so long and so hard in all my life. I just kept crying and asking God why. And when I thought I was too exhausted to cry anymore or that there were no tears left to cry, I continued. The pain and tears were coming from the deepest places of my soul.

"In the same way, the Spirit helps us in our weakness. We do not know what we ought to pray for, but the Spirit himself intercedes for us with groans that words cannot express." Romans 8:26

I was drained, physically, emotionally, spiritually. I had nothing left. I felt nothing. It was all too much for me to bear. I wanted to die. I wanted to escape from this horrible nightmare, to wake up and be holding Joshua and know that it had not been real. But I could not. It was too painful to feel, so my body went numb and blank. It was the only way I knew to cope. I truly don't remember any of the next few days except Bill making me take a shower and dragging me to the grocery store to get me out of the house. Looking back on those days, I feel a tremendous amount of guilt. Bill was dealing with the same pain and loss as I was. Joshua was his so, too. But yet, he was forced to take care of me. I had shut down. He told me later how worried he had been for me and how difficult it was for him to see me in that state. He told me all I did was sit in our bed and rock back and forth. He wasn't able to deal with his hurt because he needed to see me through mine. He is a very strong person. He demonstrated genuine and true love to me, putting aside his own pressing needs and putting me first. He is the most unselfish person I know. At this point, I knew that my strength was gone. There was nothing I was able to do on my own. It was God's strength and power that carried me through this dark time when I could not see. I was the weakest I had ever been. How wonderful and amazing that God never grows weary or tired and is always there to wrap us in His arms and carry us.

"Be still before the Lord and wait patiently for Him." Psalm 37:7

"Be still, and know that I am God." Psalm 46:10

19
OUR REUNION

On Thursday evening, our lawyer came by the house and brought us back our car seat. I thank God for him. He showed us compassion and went above and beyond what was expected from him. He stayed for a while and we talked, but I have no recollection about what. After he left, we received a phone call from Sam's step dad. Our blood pressures sky rocketed when we saw the number on our caller ID. Bill listened to the message he left. He said he had important information regarding the baby. Bill called our lawyer, who had given us his home phone number thankfully, and asked him to call to find out what they wanted. Our lawyer called us back fairly quickly. He said Sam did not want to keep the baby. She had had a taste of motherhood and didn't like it. They didn't want to keep Josh another night and wanted us to come and get him. We could not get excited or too hopeful. We were of course happy with the idea of being able to hold Josh again, but we were so very guarded. We did not want to bring him back into our home until the papers had been signed by Sam terminating her parental rights. We made a phone call once again to the wonderful foster family who had kept him just one night before. It was late, probably 8:00 or so at night. We knew we were asking a lot of this family, but trusted that God would make a way. She was very kind and very happy to help out. Our lawyer had said he was pretty certain he could get Sam to court on Friday so it would just be for one night. We decided that we would go to Sam's house and pick Joshua up and take him to the foster home for the night. I needed to see him and kiss him and hold him.

It was about a forty-five minute drive to Sam's. It was a long time to be just be sitting with all of our thoughts and feelings and fears. Neither of us talked. I wasn't sure how I would react when we got to her house and I saw her. Would I punch her or would I yell at her? I had no idea. Thankfully, God was in control and interceded. Otherwise, I may have been arrested for murder. When we pulled into the driveway, Sam met us outside carrying Josh. She gave him to me right away and apologized several times. I did speak to her, but it was kind and gentle-God given. We walked inside and talked for a few minutes. It was very calm and peaceful. They had already gathered up his things and seemed surprisingly ready to let him go. There were no tears from Sam or her mother, quite different from the last time I had seen them at the hospital. Bill talked with her step dad for a few minutes on the porch. He said that he and her mom had made it clear to Sam that she was going to be responsible for taking care of Josh. She was going to be the one to change his diapers and get up during the night to feed him and soothe him when he cried. She was expected to keep him in her room and be the mom. I guess one night was all Sam needed to realize that she wasn't ready or willing to be the mom. She seemed very confident when she handed him back to me, a confidence I hadn't seen before. We said goodbye and left. They did not know that we were taking Josh to the foster home that night. They didn't know we had taken him there the night before.

It was probably after ten that night before we arrived at the foster home. I can't say enough how blessed we were by that dear lady. God allowed her to be a part of this incredible journey. We felt like we had known her for so long, yet we had never met her face to face. We immediately felt comfortable with her and totally at peace leaving Josh in her care. We talked for close to an hour about Sam and about our situation. Before we left, she prayed with us and gave us hope. We drove home that night with trusting hearts. We knew that God was bringing us back together to be a family and that we had to rely on Him and follow His lead.

Friday morning, we waited for a phone call from our lawyer saying that Sam had signed the papers. He was going to pick her up himself from her house and drive her downtown to court. Again, God provided. We got the call! He said everything had gone smoothly and that Sam signed the papers without any hesitation or tears. She knew she was doing the right thing for Josh and for herself. We were able to go and pick up our son! What a blessed and happy reunion!!!! It had been a rough ride, but I would do it all again to be able to look into those adorable little eyes and hold those precious hands and call him "my son."

What a long journey!!! We had no idea when we first made the decision to try to have a family that God would lead us down the road He did. We expected a smooth and easy ride, just like so many others. We assumed my body would work and we would have nine months of pure joy and giddy excitement before God blessed us with a precious baby to love. He did grant us the desire of our hearts, but He chose to do it in a very different way than we would have chosen. The funny thing is I would go through it all again in a heartbeat knowing it would mean Joshua was at the end of the journey. I love him more than I hated the pain. The pain was temporary. My love for my son is forever. He was worth the journey. He is worth a thousand journeys. It is humbling to me to think that even before Bill and I were conceived, God knew that we were going to be Joshua's parents. He knew that He would bring us together to be a family. We needed Josh and Josh needed us. It is perfect.

"As for God, his way is perfect." Psalm 18:30

20
EMPATHY

I titled this book "The Gifts of Infertility" because there are several gifts that I received from this unexpected journey. When you are on a difficult road, it's sometimes impossible to see the good or the gifts that can be gleaned from going through the trial. God places difficult circumstances in our lives for different reasons, one of which I believe is to help us grow. It is important that we not only stay strong in our faith through these times, but also to be able to walk away on the other side of the trial being able to recognize the gifts we received as a result. One of those gifts that I have received is empathy. I now have first hand knowledge of how people who are grieving feel. I have been on the other side of the glass wall staring out as the world continues to speed by, not noticing that I am screaming and bleeding. No one hears. No one sees. Their world has not stopped. My grief has not affected their daily life. It doesn't mean they do not care. It simply means they are living their lives, maybe unaware of the hurt around them or maybe not wanting to see the ugliness or not knowing how to help. I know that feeling of isolation and abandonment. I try now to notice when someone is behind that wall of grief, suffering alone and trying to cope with the reality of their loss. I understand that what they want and need most is a hug and to know someone cares and realizes their pain. They want desperately for someone to reach out. That's it. I've learned that there's no need for me to struggle with trying to find the right words that will make their pain lighter or go away. It can't be done. No matter what I say, their pain is going to continue to be there and sting and burn. I've learned that I do not need to feel uncomfortable and therefore avoid the person because I don't know what to say or what to do. I've learned all I need to do is simply be. When people tried to be my counselor, preacher, or therapist, they usually ended up making me angry. Their comments, more often than not, made me feel as if they were trying to minimize my grief. "It'll be okay. Just put on a smile, remember God loves you, and you'll be fine." I've learned what people need most when they've had the rug pulled out from under them is a gentle, loving friend who can say, "I'm so sorry you are going through this. I can't imagine how hard it is." And then let the person who is grieving talk about their grief and their situation. I've learned to not reverse the roles. They don't want to hear about my story or my friend's neighbor's story. They need to be listened to, not forced to be the listener. I've also learned that they need to not feel threatened. If they are afraid I'm going to judge them or try to paint a sunny picture over their storm of gray and black, they are not going to feel free to share their thoughts and feelings. I have to convey to them that I've learned I need to allow them to feel what they feel, that their healing will come with time, but that initially they want me to stand with them, arms around them, in the middle of the storm. I need to cry with them and hold them while the rain falls and the thunder crashes and the wind blows. Healing can not happen if one avoids the storm. I tried that. I tried hiding under a rock to avoid the pelting and stinging of the storm. But I learned I had to run out into the open and face the storm head on. I needed to be exposed and naked, stripped of the clothes used to try to hide my raw and ugly wounds.

The words of the Third Day song "When the rain comes" have a deeper meaning to me now. To me, it speaks to being there for your friend when the storms hit. Not trying to say just the right words, tell them how they should feel or make the storms seem less powerful and destructive, but just being there and holding them and letting them know you care.

"Praise be to the God and Father of our Lord Jesus Christ, the Father of compassion and the God of all comfort, who comforts us in all our troubles, so that we can comfort those in any trouble with the comfort we ourselves have received from God." 2 Corinthians 1:3-4

21
HONESTY

Another gift I received from my journey of infertility is honesty-- honesty with myself and honesty with others. I learned that I can not hide from my feelings and emotions and pain. I discovered that I can not make feelings go away just by ignoring them and pretending that they do not exist. I can maybe succeed temporarily, but not for the long haul. Feelings need to be dealt with, and it is best to deal with them initially rather than letting them stew and boil and grow and fester.

It is not an easy task to bring those ugly and unpleasant emotions to the surface and out in the open. It is painful to face them and to talk about them. It is hard to admit to yourself that you need help, especially when most everyone in your circle of family and friends does not understand your pain and struggles. But the work needs to be done. The work is inevitable if we are to lead lives that are happy and free of emotional struggles. So journal, pray, find a support group, talk to a therapist, read books. Do anything, no matter how small, to begin embracing those feelings and claiming ownership of them.

I also learned to be honest with people around me who love and care for me. As much as I would like for it to be true, they can't read my mind. Yes, it would've been so nice and much easier if my family just knew when some situation was hard for me or if they truly understood the intensity of my pain and heartache. But that was not the case. They are not going to know unless I tell them. Even if the moments of having to verbalize all that I am feeling bring tears and difficulty in trying to explain, the reward will be worth it when they can then help and sympathize with me. I did give my mom and my sister a book to read at some point. It was a book written by a woman who had suffered through several miscarriages and it documented her struggles. It was effort on my part, but I left it at that. I guess the book was at least a start, but it was a story of someone else. It did not tell them the story of me and my battles. Looking back, I should've talked to them after they read the book and used it as a way to open a discussion about how I related to her story, of how some of my struggles were similar and how some were different. I needed to let them see into MY life.

Sharing and being honest with others is so helpful in two ways. One, just talking about how you feel and letting it all out, including the tears, is healing in its own way. Keeping things bottled up inside is like shaking a soda bottle with the lid on---eventually it will explode! Then watch out whoever is in the line of fire!!!!! That happened to my friend that I wrote about. She told me she was expecting and off came my lid. She then became the target of months and months of pent up anger and resentment. I am blessed that she was able to understand that the fire was not meant for her, but that she was the closest thing I could hit. God bless her for still being willing to be my friend. I hope I am the friend to her that she has been to me!

Second, being open and honest with people lets them know where you are and what you are struggling with. Then, hopefully, they will be able to provide more love and support and understanding. It will help them see into your daily life and realize that some days are just too hard to face. They will hopefully understand that even the smallest of things can trigger tears and a downward spiral that can take days to recover. It will help you not feel so alone.

Of course, you can only be as honest as you know how. Take my friend Ann, for instance. It had never occurred to me to ask her to let me know through a third party if she ever became pregnant. I had no idea that they were trying to start a family, so that particular thought would never have come to my mind. However, if I had been more honest and shared more with her in the months before that, maybe she would've suspected that news of her being pregnant would be difficult for me to hear from her. It's always easier to hear upsetting news like that from someone else so that you have time to digest it before you have to respond to that person. She didn't know that. Neither did I. Now I can hopefully help you dear friend. Share, talk, discuss, cry, scream. Your family and friends love you so much and want to help you.

22
STRONGER MARRIAGE

A third gift that I have received is a stronger marriage. That is not always the case. Sometimes the stress and financial burden and emotional warfare is too much for couples and they end up deciding to divorce. Sadly, sometimes the desire for children outweighs the commitment to stay together till death, and people move on to someone else who they believe will be able to provide for them the one thing they are consumed by.... offspring. Fortunately, we were able to weather the storm and emerge stronger and closer. God saw us through and has blessed us. I'm not saying it wasn't rough at times. The emotional stress was overwhelming. Bill did not understand all that I was struggling with, mostly because I did not share with him. He probably felt helpless not knowing what I needed or how to help. It was impossible to have any kind of meaningful intimacy during those years. Sex had simply become a means to an end. We made love when the calendar said it was the right time to conceive. I went through the motions. Any other time of the month, I rarely had the interest or the emotional energy. Love making became a chore I had to perform, not a way to express my love to my husband. And there were, of course, very dry spells after each pregnancy and surgery when intimacy was non-existent. I know this was difficult for Bill. I was just going through the days doing what I HAD to do and nothing more. He never knew when I was going to burst into tears or how he would find me when he walked in the door after a long day at work. No one, not even me, ever asked him how he was doing or how he was feeling. God bless him for sticking it out and standing by my side. He kept his promise of "for worse" for several years. He was living with a woman who was tortured and weary. He did not place blame on me for not being able to give him children. I did that every day a dozen times, enough for me and him. He would say every so often, just at a time when I needed to hear it, that if we never had children, he was okay with that, as long as we had each other. He indeed treasured me over the desire to have children. A family was something he wanted, but he wanted me first. I give him most of the credit for keeping us strong day after day. He has such a quiet strength and a gentle loving spirit. I would never have made it through had it not been for his constant presence and tenderness. We are stronger than we were. Our vows were put to the test--for better, for worse. We've seen each other at our lowest and most vulnerable. But we clung to each other and loved each other more. We are stronger now because we have witnessed first hand the action backing up the words. Our vows have a deeper meaning. We know that the other person is not going anywhere. We withstood standing naked and unprotected out in the storm and made it! We now know that we can get through any other storm that passes over us. All we need to do is hang on tightly to each other and trust God to see us through.

"O Lord my God, I take refuge in you." Psalm 7:1

23
STRONGER FAITH
AND WITNESS

The most precious gift I have received is that of a stronger faith. Never before had I come face to face with such difficult questions about God. Never had I experienced the feeling of abandonment from Him and also sensed His presence and care more strongly. I was forced to take a hard look at my faith and what I believed. I had to blindly follow Him and trust in His ways because that's all I had. My life was spinning out of control. I certainly had no control over what was happening. Nothing made sense. Not even God. But I knew down in the deepest part of my heart that He was there beside me, holding my hand and gently leading me to the place He wanted me to go. I didn't like the path He had chosen to get me to that place, but I knew He loved me and trusted that He knew best. His ways are perfect, even if we don't understand them. I learned that God is more concerned with our hearts, attitude, and growth than our present circumstances.

"In this you greatly rejoice, though now for a little while you may have had to suffer grief in all kinds of trials. These

have come so that your faith-of greater worth than gold, which perishes even though refined by fire-may be proved genuine and may result in praise, glory and honor when Jesus Christ is revealed." 1 Peter 1:6-7 This doesn't mean He doesn't want us to be happy. God loves His children. He wants to give us the desires of our hearts, if those desires are pure and right and pleasing to Him. But God is more interested in the health of our faith, in the condition of our heart. God is more interested in the eternal than the temporary. *"I consider that our present sufferings are not worth comparing with the glory that will be revealed in us." Romans 8:18* God uses situations and circumstances to teach us and to hopefully draw us closer to Him. I am a stronger, more grounded Christian now because of these experiences. I've seen God in action. Before this journey, I would read about God's love and provision in the Scriptures. I would read about His love and His promise to never leave us, but it was just words I read. I believed it as much as I could at the time. But now those words have come alive! I truly understand what they mean, and I cling to them each and every day. I know, without a shadow of a doubt, that God is there all the time, even when He chooses to be silent. I know that He will provide what I need, when I need it, and I need to be thankful. I am not frightened of the future and all of the things that could go wrong. I have a steady peace and hope that whatever this world may throw at me, I will be able to handle it and make it through because of the strength and the love of the God who calls me His child.

No one wants to suffer or go through trials. I've never met anyone yet who prays for a hardship in their life because things have been going along too smoothly. I've never met anyone who enjoys the pain and uncertainty of a trial. I have learned that the trials will come. There will certainly be situations in our time here on earth that are difficult and unpleasant. God never said our lives would be easy and free of pain, not even to His children. He did say that He would be with us, holding us and guiding us when those times come. His desire is for us to reach out to Him and draw closer to Him during those times, to realize that we need His strength and wisdom and direction, and hopefully bring glory to Him. I have drawn closer to God through this season of suffering. I've learned that I can not blame God when life does not happen the way I wanted or planned it to. It is not His fault. He is not responsible for sitting on His throne willing bad things to happen to us. He does, however, use those circumstances to teach and to discipline. I've learned that life is only a small part of what happens to me and a huge part of how I respond to it. That does not mean that I subscribe to the "Jesus loves you…just be happy and get over it" philosophy. Not at all. We are human, and therefore we have human emotions that need to be recognized and dealt with. Being a Christian does not mean that you do not grieve. It means you grieve with hope. It means you are able to see, at some point, the bigger picture, not just the single puzzle piece. It means that as Christians, we cry and scream and talk and journal and all of the other things that we need to do to get through a terrible situation. But at the end of the day, we have the hope that all of our pain and sadness is a grain of sand compared to the happiness and joy we will have once we reach our home in Heaven. What a glorious thought!!!!! We need to keep our eyes fixed on Jesus! We need to not give Satan the foothold to make us doubt and blame and stray from the God who loves us so much.

I've also learned that God's purpose trumps my purpose. I should approach trials with the attitude of recognizing that God's purpose needs to be a priority to me. I should not focus on seeing just the single puzzle piece and thinking it unfair when God created and can see the entire puzzle. I need to remember that I am not God, I am His creation. Having faith is easy when things are sailing along and there isn't any trial or difficult circumstance. Having faith when we are faced with pain and grief and suffering takes growth and experiences and commitment. It is something that comes with time and maturity as a Christian. I am reminded of the story of a tree all alone out in a field. It grows every year as it's roots reach deeper into the ground and it's branches and leaves reach upward to the sky. The storms come and the tree is made to bend with the mighty wind and the pelting rain as it sways and withstands the harsh weather. But these storms force the tree to grow stronger and deeper roots so that when the next storms come, it will be stronger and better equipped to handle whatever the storm has to throw at it. It is the same with us as Christians. If things were always easy and smooth, our faith would be stagnate, there would be nothing to challenge it and encourage it to grow. We need the storms to come so that our faith will become stronger and deeper, just like that old tree.

I also need to have a heart and attitude of worship even when I do not feel like it. It's not about me, it's about giving God what He deserves. And God deserves my worship and praise even when things in this life are rough and not going the way I want. He is my father.

I also feel as if I understand prayer a little more, though I admit it is still a subject where I have much more to learn! There were days and sometimes weeks during my stay in the pit that I felt it useless to pray. I gave up. I asked others to pray instead because I couldn't do it anymore. God was not answering my prayers the way I wanted Him to, so I was frustrated and angry. I was not getting what I wanted, when I wanted it. I was stomping my foot at God and accusing Him of not listening to me and of not caring about me and my heart's desires. If Jesus would have been here, physically, standing next to me, He would have made me sit in time out until my attitude was adjusted!

Looking back on that experience and having the hindsight to see what God was doing, I now understand that God always hears our prayers. He may not answer them the way we would want Him to. Sometimes the answer is painful and miserable. Sometimes the answer is to wait, to be still and wait for His perfect timing. A very wise Christian woman wrote on Joshua's message picture frame at our baby shower the simple yet powerful phrase, "in His time." I think of that often, even now, when I pray. He knows how many hairs I have on my head. He can see all of the choices I will make from now until I draw my last breath. He knows what I need, and I trust that He will bring that in His time, not mine. He is the creator of all things, the omniscient and all powerful God. He is most capable of taking care of my needs and my wants and He does not need my help in doing it.

I also hope that I am a stronger witness for the Lord, not only for the story I can share but also for the life I lead. Our life is a sermon to others every day. People are constantly watching how we respond to situations and difficulties, observing our attitudes and listening to our words. I hope that when I am faced with difficult and trying circumstances, the world sees my response as one who has an inner peace and a steadfast faith. I want to be a light for the One who sustains me and for the One who is my hope and strength. I want the world to see something different in me. Yes, there are trials and tribulations that I will face. There will be more heartaches and sadness that lie in my future. But I want to be able to see the bigger picture and to always remember that these hurts on earth are temporary. I will bend and sway with the storm when it comes, just like the old tree, but come out on the other side of it hopefully a stronger witness for what God can do and does do if we acknowledge His provision. I must remember that God loves me so very much and if He sets a road before me, even one that I would not have chosen on my own, I need to go down that road because He wants me to. He will not send me down the road by myself. He promises to walk right beside me, holding my hand and guiding me. I simply have to trust and follow. Whatever bumps and valleys there are along the way, God will see me through.

"But we also rejoice in our sufferings, because we know that suffering produces perseverance; perseverance, character; and character, hope." Romans 5:3–4

24
ACCEPTANCE

I have learned to accept a few things out of my healing. I've learned to accept my scars, my emotional scars. I used to try to cover them, to hide them and keep them out of sight. I didn't want anyone to know about them or ask about them. They were to me a mark of failure. Not anymore. Now I accept the scars as a part of me. I am proud of them. I would not be where I am today if it weren't for them. They are daily reminders of where I have been and how God has healed me. Some of the scars are still tender and can become easily irritated and sore. I received one of these scars as a result of never being pregnant and never having had the experience of giving birth. I have accepted that truth, but it is still painful at times to hear a woman sharing her happy news with others. I still find it difficult to be around pregnant people and to listen to them talk about the joys and pains of pregnancy and their anticipation of giving birth. I was at a meeting at our church recently and the conversation somehow turned to everyone sharing in their labor and birth stories. I just sat and listened. A part of my heart began to feel the weight and ache of that scar. I could not join in the conversation. I felt very isolated and, for a brief moment, I felt the sting of being a failure again. My body was not able to do the very thing for which it was designed. The old enemies of bitterness and self pity began to creep back and take hold. But I realized what Satan was trying to do, and I prayed for God's help to overcome those nasty feelings. I don't know how long that particular scar will be sensitive and easily opened. It may never heal completely. It may always be a chore for me to go to a baby shower or for me to hear a friend is expecting. I accept that. I pray that over the years, it will become easier.

I've also learned to accept that miscarriages are very misunderstood by the general public. People who have not experienced a miscarriage for themselves typically do not comprehend the time it takes to heal. They expect a few days of mourning and then for us to get on with our lives. I assume that is because, in their eyes, there was never a "baby" to see and hold. It was just a clump of tissue that obviously wasn't healthy. They don't understand the depth of the grief and pain one feels when a life, no matter how small, is lost. And I've accepted that to expect anything different is unrealistic. I can not begin to imagine the pain of losing my husband, the day to day, step by step struggle to continue on living without him by my side. I can reach out to a widow, show her love and compassion, but I can not know what her heart is feeling and know the difficulty in coping with her loss. We can't expect people to fully grasp and understand a circumstance that they themselves have not had to endure. It was not fair of me to expect my family and close friends to realize all of the little battles that were waged during my emotional war.

How would they know? I can now, however, help people to understand when the situation presents itself. I can be open about my experience and pray that it will help others better minister to those who are hurting.

But most importantly, I've learned to accept my infertility. I accept that this is who I am. I still do not have a firm grip on the answer to the question, "Did God create me this way or was it just happenstance?" Does He intentionally create someone without eyesight or without a limb? Do those things just occur as a result of nature? I don't know. Maybe God did create me unable to bear children. Maybe it was just a result of my body not working the way it was supposed to. Perhaps God created me with the inability to bear children because He knew my infertility would be the vessel used to draw me closer to Him and to see things more clearly. It doesn't matter. This is how I am, whether God planned it that way or not. He still created me and loves me. *"For you created my inmost being; you knit me together in my mother's womb. I praise you because I am fearfully and wonderfully made; your works are wonderful, I know that full well. My frame was not hidden from you when I was made in the secret place. When I was woven together in the depths of the earth, your eyes saw my unformed body. All the days ordained for me were written in your book before one of them came to be." Psalm 139:13–16* My infertility brought Josh into our hearts and lives. So when I look at it from that perspective, I am exactly the way I needed to be.

25
THANKFULNESS

The last gift I received is that of thankfulness. God has taught me to be thankful in all situations. That, of course, does not mean I am expected to jump for joy when a trial comes and run through the streets singing. It lies on a deeper level than that. It means having the attitude of thankfulness for everything we have and for all situations because we know and trust that God is working in our lives and that His purpose is being established. It means that we pause in the midst of the storm to see God's hand and to recognize and acknowledge that He is with us. It means that I am thankful for my infertility because the grief, suffering and pain that came with it has made me stronger. It deepened my faith. It led us to adoption. It led us to Josh. My infertility led me to being a mom. I am truly thankful.

26
WHERE I AM NOW

As I am writing this chapter, it has been almost nine years since that trip to Lake Erie for my birthday and our decision was made to begin trying for a family. It seems like just yesterday. It seems like a thousand years ago. I can still remember certain events from this journey with such clarity and recollection of detail. There are frames of time frozen in my mind. The nurse waving the pregnancy stick telling me I'm pregnant for the first time; the look on the ultrasound technician's face when she couldn't find our baby's heartbeat; exactly where I was sitting and what I was doing when the lawyer called to ask me if we were still interested in adopting; the sights and smells of walking into the nursery and seeing our son for the first time.

I am happy and in full swing of being a little boy's mother. I love the feeling of having his little hand in mine, the sound of "mommy" coming from his little voice, and the joy I feel when we are together as a family experiencing something from his perspective. It is an amazing thing to be called mama. Our family is complete. We had wanted a sibling for Joshua, but for His reason and plan, God did not bring another child into our life. Bill has had a vasectomy and our home study has expired. They were steps that we took over a period of three years. I could not close the door all at once. It was a very difficult thing to acknowledge that I was never going to have a biological child. I have accepted it, but it still haunts me at times. The basement still has a corner devoted to the storage of baby clothes, swings, car seats, high chairs and bouncy seats. My head knows that we are finished with these things, that I need to pass them on to someone else who could use them. And yet I can't find the strength to clear it out. It's like a death. I know it will be emotional saying goodbye to the sweet baby clothes and the baby gear that represented such a precious and short chapter in our lives only to be played out one time. But I will get there. I know I need to do it on my time schedule, when I feel ready. That could be tomorrow. That could be when I'm fifty. I may end up keeping it all for our grandchildren. Whatever I decide, it will be the right time, for me.

We do not have a relationship with Sam, as of now. During the first year of Josh's life, she called several times and we would send her letters with updates and pictures of Josh. She has not seen him since that night when we drove to her house to pick him up. We have not heard from her in several years. Maybe we will some day. I do not hold any bitterness in my heart toward her for taking Josh back. She was only a child herself forced to make a very difficult and mature decision. I think that maybe she had to have him for a night to find out on her own that she was not ready to be someone's mother. If that is what she needed to be able to have peace for the rest of her life that she made the right decision, then that's how it had to be.

I still pray for her and thank God that she chose life for her baby and that she placed him in my arms.

I still cringe when I hear the term miscarriage. It still makes my heart ache, for myself and for the women who are enduring the pain today. I still feel angry when I see young teenage girls who are pregnant or I hear about someone getting pregnant when they didn't want to. I still find it difficult to listen to stories about giving birth. I still dread going to the OB/GYN every year for my check up and exam and seeing the waiting room full of expectant mothers rubbing their baby bump bellies and hearing them talk about their pregnancy joys and pains. The good thing is that I am aware of all of these things and my feelings towards them. I know what to expect from these situations and I know that the feelings I have are valid and that I can deal with them. They do not run my life anymore. When my scars become irritated, I rub them and tend to them. They heal, and I move on.

So that is my story. The experiences I have shared have molded and shaped me into the person I am today. I am changed forever. I have been broken and restored. Rocked to the core. Felt the heaviness and weight of grief and hopelessness and felt the relief and freedom from it being lifted. I have been buried in the pit of grief and hopelessness and thought I didn't have the strength or will to claw my way out. I have felt the warm sunlight on my soul as I emerged from that pit and began to shake off the dirt and grime from the years of misery and pain.

I have scars that will always be with me. They are a part of me. I did not ask for them, but I would not trade them. They remind me daily of where I have been and of what God has done with my life. So does our son, Joshua. He is a blessing, a reminder of how precious life is and of the journey we were put on to find him. He is not ours. He is a gift. One of the many gifts of my infertility.

10 TIPS FOR HEALTHY GRIEVING
By Steve Arterburn
New Life Ministries

1. **Stay "connected" with someone**. Find a trusted friend, pastor or counselor with whom you can be real. Speak what's on your mind and in your heart. If this feels one-sided, let that be okay for this period of your life. Chances are the other person will find meaning in what they're doing. And the time will come when you'll have the chance to be a good listener for someone else. You'll be a better listener then if you're a good talker now.

2. **Don't be afraid to tell people what helps you and what doesn't**. People around you may not understand what you need-so tell them. If you need more time alone, or assistance with chores you're unable to complete, or an occasional hug, be honest. People can't read your mind, so you'll have to speak it.

3. **Invite someone to be your telephone buddy**. If your grief and sadness hit you especially

hard at times and you have no one nearby to turn to, ask someone you trust to be your telephone buddy. Ask their permission for you to call them whenever you feel you're in trouble, day or night. Then put their number beside your phone and call them if you need them.

4. **Journal**. Write out your thoughts, feelings and prayers. Be as honest as you can. In time, go back through your writings and notice how you're changing and growing. Write about that to.

5. **Write the person who died**. Write a letter to your loved one, thoughts you wish you could express if they were present. This can be a key step in coming to terms with your feelings and bringing a degree of healing closure.

6. **Consider a church or community grief support group**. You were not created to be alone all the time. Gathering with others who've experienced similar loss can remove the isolation so often associated with grief.

7. **Plant something living as a memorial**. Plant a flower, a bush or a tree in memory of the one who died. Or plant several things. Do this ceremonially if you wish, perhaps with others present. If you do this planting where you live, you can watch it grow and change day by day, season by season. You can even make

it a part of special times of remembrance in the future.

8. **Give yourself permission to change some things**. As soon as it seems right, alter some things in your home to make clear this significant change that has occurred. Rearrange a room or replace a piece of furniture or give away certain items that will never again be used. This doesn't mean to remove all signs of the one who died, but, preserving a "shrine" to your lost loved one can be harmful, in that it may not allow for the closure process to begin.

9. **Allow yourself to laugh and cry**. Sometimes something funny will happen to you, just like it used to. When that happens, go ahead and laugh if it feels funny to you. You won't be desecrating your loved one's memory. Crying goes naturally with grief. Tears well up and fall even when you least expect them. It may feel awkward to you, but this is not unusual for a person in your situation. A good rule of thumb is this: if you feel like crying, then cry.

10. **Do something to help someone else**. Step out of your own problems from time to time and devote your attention to someone else. Offer a gift or your service. Placing your focus on someone else will help you avoid the traps of self pity and anger.

"A PAIR OF SHOES"
Author unknown

I am wearing a pair of shoes. They are ugly shoes. Uncomfortable shoes. I hate my shoes. Each day I wear them, and each day I wish I had another pair. Some days my shoes hurt so bad that I do not think I can take another step. Yet, I continue to wear them. I get funny looks wearing these shoes. They are looks of sympathy. I can tell in others eyes that they are glad they are my shoes and not theirs. They never talk about my shoes. To learn how awful my shoes are might make them uncomfortable. To truly understand these shoes you must walk in them. But, once you put them on, you can never take them off. I now realize that I am not the only one who wears these shoes. There are many pairs in this world. Some women are like me and ache daily as they try and walk in them. Some have learned how to walk in them so they don't hurt quite as much. Some have worn the shoes so long that days will go by before they think about how much they hurt. No woman deserves to wear these shoes. Yet, because of these shoes I am a stronger woman. These shoes have given me the strength to face anything. They have made me who I am. I will forever walk in the shoes of a woman who has lost a child.